FOR BUSINESS

A Quick Start Guide to
GOOGLE ADWORDS

NEW TOOLS
FOR
BUSINESS

A Quick Start Guide to
GOOGLE ADWORDS

How to get your product to
the top of Google and reach
your customers

Mark Harnett

KoganPage

LONDON PHILADELPHIA NEW DELHI

First published in Great Britain and the United States in 2010 by Kogan Page Limited

Apart from any fair dealing for the purposes of research or private study, or criticism or review, as permitted under the Copyright, Designs and Patents Act 1988, this publication may only be reproduced, stored or transmitted, in any form or by any means, with the prior permission in writing of the publishers, or in the case of reprographic reproduction in accordance with the terms and licences issued by the CLA. Enquiries concerning reproduction outside these terms should be sent to the publishers at the undermentioned addresses:

120 Pentonville Road	525 South 4th Street, #241	4737/23 Ansari Road
London N1 9JN	Philadelphia PA 19147	Daryaganj
United Kingdom	USA	New Delhi 110002
www.koganpage.com		India

© Mark Harnett, 2010

The right of Mark Harnett to be identified as the author of this work has been asserted by him in accordance with the Copyright, Designs and Patents Act 1988.

ISBN   978 0 7494 6003 7
E-ISBN   978 0 7494 6004 4

British Library Cataloguing-in-Publication Data

A CIP record for this book is available from the British Library.

Library of Congress Cataloging-in-Publication Data

Harnett, Mark.
    A quick start guide to Google AdWords : get your product to the top of Google and reach your customers / Mark Harnett.
        p. cm.
    ISBN 978-0-7494-6003-7 — ISBN 978-0-7494-6004-4   1. Google AdWords.
2. Internet marketing.   I. Title.
    HF5415.1265.H374 2010
    659.14'4—dc22

                                                                    2010016131

Typeset by Graphicraft Limited, Hong Kong
Printed and bound in India by Replika Press Pvt Ltd

CONTENTS

INTRODUCTION

Using Google AdWords is as easy as writing a small advertisement on a postcard to put in your local newsagents window. The only difference is that while the postcard will only be read by the people who visit the newsagent, the advertisement you write and put online can be read by millions of people all over the world. With the newsagent you use sticky tape to place the postcard on the window. With Google AdWords you choose a word to describe what you are selling. If it is the same word that someone who wants to buy from you is using in their search for the product, then they will find your advertisement. This book is packed with stories of people who are running successful businesses using Google AdWords to bring customers to their websites. Choose a story that is similar to your business and copy what they did. It's easy!

CHAPTER 1
THE QUICK START

In the next few pages you are going to learn how to:

- Set up your **AdWords Account**.

- Create a **web page** ready for your buyers to visit,
  which will have:
  — a domain name;
  — a web host;
  — your design.

- Keep your expenditure within control by using the
  Budget optimizer key.

- Write an Ad and understand how to choose a
  Keyword.

- Write more ads using the **Create Another Ad** variation.

- Run the **Keyword selector** tool so you know which are
  popular keywords.

- Understand the **Control panel** so that you can see how
  your Ad is performing.

CASE STUDY

Using Quick Start because you don't have time

HOLIDAY HOME RENTAL

This is a case study about a man who is time poor, but had a problem to solve. His name is Robin and he's the owner of a mountain cabin in the Canadian Rockies. Robin is time poor because he's a city broker in Calgary, Alberta and he spends his weekends and evenings mountain climbing or skiing in the Rockies. He doesn't spend his precious leisure time worrying about AdWords, because he has found a way to use Google to make money while he's out trekking in the mountains. He's not interested in sitting at home behind a computer, so he uses Google AdWords to have more time to spend in the wilderness.

Robin decided five years ago to rent out his cabin in the Rockies at the times when he wasn't using it himself. He knew there was no point in putting a 'For Rent' notice hanging from the door of the cabin because it isn't close to a main road; it's up a long track in the middle of nowhere. So he prepared a printed brochure and gave it to the tourist office in his nearest small town, Golden, British Columbia. Nothing happened. No one rented.

Then Robin spent a week of late nights, after work in the city, building his own website; putting up pictures of the cabin and describing how it has four bedrooms and great views of the mountains. He could have used a web designer but he enjoyed doing it himself. At the same time he paid $100 Canadian to a home rentals website that listed his cabin as a holiday rental; he told me, 'The companies that work as a compendium of individual owners have "three month free listing" introductory offers on their websites, so I posted my site details on several other rental sites.'

This was a smart idea because links to other websites help lift your website listing in the organic or non-sponsored part of the Google search engine. But that wasn't enough to create traffic to his website and help him rent out the cabin.

When Robin returned from one of his many adventurous mountain trips, he took my Quick Guide advice and registered with Google AdWords. Then he sat round with some climbing friends and a few beers and made a list of all the AdWords that would attract interest in the cabin from potential renters. He says, 'It was an animated discussion and we listed lots of ideas. We thought of all the words holidaymakers might search for, like ski holiday homes, cabin home, mountain biking cabin, British Columbia cabins, Golden vacations, and many other iterations.'

The great thing about Google AdWords is that it's very simple. Robin knew he should drop any words that didn't work and within a few days realized that 'all of them were useless.' Of course he didn't have to pay for the words that were no good because no one had clicked on them.

Over the following months, Robin experimented with more words until he discovered the three keywords to bring visitors to his website and ensure his cabin is now full with paying visitors all the year round. He said, 'I pay for three words – Golden, BC and Golden British Columbia, which gives me 600 hits a month. I know there is lots of complexity of the AdWords that could have been used, but I'm not interested. I don't want to bother.'

Robin has continued to use the same three keywords and just one advertisement that hasn't changed.

His headline is 'Golden BC Vacation Home' and 'Spectacular private 4 bedroom house in the Rocky Mountains. www.holidayhome.ca' is the ad wording.

Today 85 per cent of his bookings come from the internet and the remainder from word of mouth and return guests.

Interestingly, when Robin started using AdWords none of his competitors were advertising online. He admits:

> I've only got 15 or 20 real vacation home competitors and then the hotels or lodges in the Golden area, and five years ago when I started doing this nobody had heard of AdWords. But now that has changed. What has happened is that the competition for the words Golden BC has increased – I started off paying 7 cents a click and now it has increased to 25 cents a click and I am one of the bottom listed advertisements on the search – so maybe the top guys are paying as much as 50 cents or even a dollar per click.

About once every couple of months Robin goes to Google.com/analytics. He clicks Access and enters his password to find more information about the people who visit the website:

> I have set my budget to 30 bucks a month, and get about 20 visitors a day. Some days are busier, for some reason Tuesdays are busiest for people looking for holidays. I can see that the average time spent on the site is a minute; and they look at 5.3 pages. Google tells me that 90 per cent are new visits and there is a great map that shows me where the visitors come from; the majority are from Canada and the USA and this month there were two from Italy and five from the UK. And looking at my customers who actually book, the ratio is the same; 80 per cent Canadian, 10 per cent American and 5 per cent from Europe.

Robin believes that the traditional holiday booking agencies are going out of business and being replaced by a whole new industry of individuals using Google AdWords to rent out their own properties.

He thinks that if you are time poor there is no need to go further than the Quick Start.

> *I could spend more time on 2nd or 3rd best keywords and play with them, but I can't be bothered; my paying clients just go my website and e-mail me or call me and that's fine with me. The cabin is good and full – 90 per cent full during peak tourist times, and just a few days empty when schedules don't fit. And it's full every weekend during the year. It's as good as it gets.*

If you can use a laptop in bed, there's no need to get out from under the duvet and you don't need to be a nerd to get started on Google AdWords.

But before you switch on your computer, ask yourself, what product or service do I want to sell?

The product or service could supply the name for your website; your domain name.

Your first task is to choose a domain name, like www.myproduct.com and set up a web page that describes your product. More details on how to do this coming up.

In less than half an hour you're going to be an internet advertising executive with new customers visiting your website, but first you need to set up a Google AdWords account and the next few pages will show you how to do it.

Your aim is to make sure that your advertisement for 'my product' is one of the top ten advertisements when a potential customer runs a Google search.

SETTING UP YOUR ADWORDS ACCOUNT

First, type 'adwords.Google.com' into your browser. Select **Try AdWords now**. The first sentence you see offers help with creating your own website. Even if you don't have one yet, ignore this as we'll come back to it a little later. Now click on **Starter Edition** and then on **Continue** at the bottom of the screen.

The first section is called **Location and Language**. Select United Kingdom, or the country where your business is based, and then let's assume you're going to do everything in English.

In the **Write your Ad** section enter the address of your website main page, which some people call the landing page as you want your customers to land on it. This address is your URL.

Now, go back to the start and check this again. It's really easy to make mistakes when you're working online. You need to check location and language and most importantly ensure that you've typed in your web address correctly; you don't want to send people to someone else's website. Congratulations, you are close to having an account!

Now let's write the AdWord copy. This is the creative bit. Enter the headline to describe 'my product' and complete the two lines of text to add further information. The headline can contain no more than 25 characters, while the two descriptive lines can contain up to 35 characters each.

Are you a words person or a numbers person? Some people find this writing part easy, but then have problems looking at the data and numbers that explain the success of the ad. If you're a numbers person don't worry. Click the link: **The five keys to powerful ads** for advice from Google about writing an effective ad. Go for it. Try to get your first draft down now and you can improve it later. This isn't like traditional advertising where you have to get the words perfect first time. You'll make more money if you're flexible; be prepared to change what you write as your skills develop.

Now you're ready to think of keywords that describe your new product. Think of just one, the most obvious word is usually the best. Write it in the text box. Put square brackets [ ] around the keyword. You do this by clicking the square brackets that are just below the minus and plus keys on the top right of the keyboard. There's more about this later in the book, but now just get going and choose your first keyword.

Choose the currency you're going to pay with, and set yourself a low monthly budget. It's a good idea to start with the sum that it would take you to buy a pair of shoes and then you can test if this works for you. In some territories Google suggests you start with a minimum figure.

Click **Continue** to go to your account and then you have a choice: if you already have an account with Google, perhaps for Gmail or spreadsheets or other Google applications, you could use the same account settings or you can create a new account. Enter your password twice and your e-mail address. Read the terms and privacy policy.

The next page will tell you to check your e-mail to verify your account. The e-mail you have been sent from Adwords will have an account number. Write it down and keep it somewhere safe with your password. Click **Continue**. Well done! You now have a Google AdWords Account.

You're going to organize your account in three simple steps. You've already completed step one: the account. Next you plan the Campaigns, then Ad Groups which contain keywords and ads. Now you have some fun things to do:

CREATING YOUR WEBSITE

There's no need to panic. Why not start with something very simple? A one page site with a description of what you plan to sell and your e-mail address and phone number so your clients can contact you from the one page. Think of it like putting a postcard in the newsagent's window, except in this case you're not dependent on everyone walking by the shop. You have the entire internet at your finger tips and no one need know you're still under the duvet.

Go back to adwords.Google.com, click the **Try AdWords now** button and this time select the link **Help me create a website with Google Sites**. Google will help you set up your own site and register your domain name.

You'll have to enter your name and address, phone number and e-mail address in the text boxes. The page will allow you to select a Google map of your location, which can be very useful if you're selling a product that is location specific; for example, if you're running a beauty salon your customers will want to see where you're based. You can also choose a Google phone number that will forward the calls to you. The good thing about this item is that Google will count the phone calls for you.

Now you've started building the website, you'll start thinking about all the extra features you want, like pictures, discussion pages, audio, video and more, but there's one key thing you must never forget.

The purpose of your site is to attract traffic

Whiz-bang features do not create traffic. You've placed a needle in a haystack. People certainly aren't just going to stumble upon your site by accident and it's unrealistic to believe that a good idea is all you need.

No one is going to find your site unless you tell people about it, and online it's not about word of mouth but about search engine appeal, so your site must appeal to the search engines. People will then visit your site because they've found it in a search.

Later on you can add the user interactivity that will make your site more appealing to customers, but now you must concentrate on the AdWords that help the search engines find your website.

The costs for a website are going to vary depending upon what you are trying to accomplish, but every website has three basic costs:

1 the domain name (myproduct.com);

2 the web host;

3 the design.

Domain names

You pay for domain names yearly and most registrars will give you a discount if you pay for multiple years. The suffix of any website indicates different information and it's usually easy to guess what they mean:

- .gov – governments or government departments, including local authorities;

- .edu – educational institutions;

- .org – organizations (usually not for profit);

- .com – the most common business address;

- .co.uk, .com.au – well, you can guess the countries.

Web hosting

A web host is the company that actually stores your web files. They allow you to publish your files to the internet and provide other features such as e-mail accounts and database support. Hosting is generally paid for with a monthly fee. Pay something like the price·of an expensive coffee and a cake per month for their smallest plan and the amount of space you'll receive is more than enough for the average customer. You can easily upgrade to a higher package should you need it. Web hosts don't help you market or optimize your site for the search engines to help you get traffic, so don't expect a lot of support from them in these areas.

Paying for a web designer

You can either learn HTML, buy some kind of web editor like Microsoft FrontPage to build your pages, or you can hire a web designer. The price of web design varies from a little to a lot. Ask friends for recommendations.

WRITING AND BUDGETING FOR YOUR ADWORDS

If that's too complicated for you, and you want to get going straight away, click on the **I don't have a web page** button. Google allows you to choose your location and the hours you want the web page to be shown, which is very useful if you are time poor like Robin, who can only talk to potential customers in the evening on his home phone number when he's back from the city. If you're going to place your office phone number on the page you might want to take the page down at certain times of the day, perhaps when you're collecting your children from school and aren't available to answer the phone.

Make sure your web page copy describes what you do. Show it to friends and ask their opinion. Google allows you to upload pictures and choose a background colour for your page. When you've finished, click **Continue** and your URL for your web page will be a Google address such as myproduct.Googlepages.com

Now your website is up and running, let's go back to the keywords you chose when you set up your account.

Type your first keyword into the Google search engine and find out who your top ten competitors are. You'll see their ads on the right hand side of the screen; sometimes the top ones are across the top of the page. If you want to know how many competitors there are then keep scrolling down the pages until you see the number one ad repeated. The total number of individual ads is the number of people who want to use that keyword.

Remember the brackets you put around the keyword? That ensures the search will only be for that exact word. You will want to type in lots of different words. That comes later. Start with one, or maybe two. If you change your mind about the keyword you have chosen, click **Delete** next to the keyword and it will be removed.

When you write the keyword into the square bracket you are asking AdWords to find you an exact match against the keyword. Try to think of the square brackets as something that creates a bucket around the word. Later in the book, I'll show you how to put lots of other words into your bucket.

Remember your monthly ad budget? You set it at the price of a pair of shoes a month. Now you have a decision to make; how much are you prepared to spend each day? If you have only a small budget then eke it out by being at the bottom of the top ten ads that are viewed by everyone all the time rather than spending it all at once by being at the top for a shorter length of time.

If you're feeling adventurous, Google has a Budget Optimizer that will give you the largest number of clicks possible for the monthly budget you have identified. You can set this for yourself by clicking on **Edit Settings** in the Control Panel and next to **Bidding**, uncheck the **Budget Optimizer**. Write in the amount you want to spend and hit the **Save** button. You can put in a very low amount and see where your ad is placed, or try for the highest sum. If you want to play safe, the Google Budget Optimizer will give you the average value for your market.

It may seem counter-intuitive, but as this is your first foray into AdWords you don't want to be the number one. Not only is it the highest price but you're also likely to have people who don't want to buy anything clicking through to your site. Every click is something you'll have to pay for. You want clicks from real buyers.

Be competitive with yourself

Have a further look at the ad you wrote ten minutes ago. Could you do better? Have another go, write a second ad and go back to your ad group and upload it. In the control panel page click the **Create Another Ad** button and on the next page select the **Variation On My Current Ad** option. When you've written it, click the **Create ad** button. This new ad will be used as an alternative to the first. Which is going to be more successful? Google will automatically test out your new ad and if it is more effective, then Google will show it more often, the system selects the top ads for you. You can have up to 50 ads at one time. So get writing.

Being competitive with yourself is called 'split testing'; a useful marketing tool that helps you identify what kind of ad will reach your customers. You can try using ads that are only slightly different and see which one works best for you.

TOP TIPS FOR FINAL QUICK START IDEAS

Be confident – It doesn't matter if you get this wrong. Every time you log into Google you can tweak your advertisement or change your keywords. It's your business and you're the advertising executive.
Feel proud of your new skill.

Get to know your control panel – When you've set up your account you'll notice a Google alert at the top of the page. You can close it if you're too busy, or read the FAQ that arrive with the new account details. When the amount of money you've placed is about to run out, then Google will use the alert to contact you.

Your ad will appear on your Control Panel looking exactly the same as it will in the search results. Click on it to make sure that you've entered the page address accurately. It's very easy to get this wrong; you don't want to send potential customers to the wrong page or even the wrong website. If you've typed in the wrong URL address, then return to AdWords and click on the **Edit** button to fix the problem. Don't forget to save your work.

The control panel shows the links that will provide the analysis your business needs to measure your AdWord success. Click on these links to find out more.

Keywords: the two words you have chosen so far.

Impressions: the number of times your ad has been displayed as a result of a search.

Clicks: the number of individual visitors clicking on your ad and arriving on your website landing page.

Total Cost: the cost per click multiplied by the number of clicks.

When you've clicked on one of the links, then information will be shown to you in a column of figures with highest numbers at the top. This is the place where the numbers experts come into their own. They may not have been happy writing the ad, but they are going to love looking at these figures. There is a **Graphs** button for you to click on the right of the screen and you can print out your graphs in Microsoft Excel. If you click on the **keyword** link again, the column will change to ascending order. This information will show you which keywords are getting the most impressions and you can start to think about how your business is performing in the market place. Read the rest of this book to improve your skills.

Question

Do you have a keyword to describe the product you are selling?

Action

Think of the words that describe your new product. Start by writing down just one – the most obvious word is best. Talk to your customers and ask them how they describe what it is you are selling. If you are a start up business and don't have any customers yet, then ask your friends. Your keyword is the essence of your Google AdWords plan.

CHAPTER 2
THE SECRET POWER OF WORDS

It doesn't take a genius to work out that the quickest and cheapest way to sell yourself or your business these days is via the internet. If you have a product or service that needs marketing, a website can put you in touch with thousands of new customers at the click of a mouse button.

But it isn't enough simply to have a web presence. How will people be drawn to your site out of the billions they could access? Here are some statistics to ponder: 100,000 new websites are built daily, and 125,000 people start a home-based business every week. So it follows that you need to find some way to make your site and your business cut through the plethora of others.

You need to advertise your product or service, or yourself, using the latest internet-based tools. This book shows you how. Doing it is cheap and easy. But there are many pitfalls. Reading the book will show you the tricks that will save you time and money.

This chapter will guide you through some of the factors you need to take into account before you set up the website that will be the shop window for you and your business, including:

- the basics of web design;

- choosing a domain name;

- building your website: templates or custom-made?

- do-it-yourself or professional?

- getting the homepage right.

CASE STUDY

Creating a website that keeps users coming back

WIGGLY WIGGLERS

Heather Gorringe is passionate about ecological lifestyle and eco-gardening. Working from her kitchen table in the family farm house, she founded Wiggly Wigglers to sell worm composting kits. As Wiggly Wigglers has expanded, she has outgrown the house and now works in several of the farm outbuildings, which she has converted for her business. Wiggly Wigglers now has a £2.5 million turnover, selling birdseed, feeders, composters, plants, flowers, turf, tools and, of course, the worms. Most products she sells are sourced locally, many from her husband Phil's farm, Lower Blakemere Farm in Herefordshire in the UK.

When Heather started off Wiggly Wigglers she was completely inexperienced in business and just wanted to 'keep going in the most wonderful part of the world'. Heather describes where she lives as having 'three times as many cows as people' so she knew she could not expect to make money selling from a farm shop. In the early days she ran a mail order company for the worm composting kits; she advertised in the specialist press and in all the national and garden magazines. She travelled the country presenting the wormeries at garden shows and trade events.

But the business remained small and she was exhausted:

The problem is that you don't wake up one morning and say I must have a worm composting set, especially when it's easier to throw your smelly kitchen waste away. You're not going to want to bring a thousand worms into your kitchen unless you really understand why a wormery is a good idea.

The internet has been a business changing tool because it provides information to potential customers. Heather decided that Wiggly Wigglers website should be a supremely useful information hub for people interested in eco-gardening. So she has packed it with specialist information about worm composting and *bokashi*, which is the Japanese composting method for kitchen waste. More importantly, she updates the content regularly. Her site has blogs, tweets, podcasts and facebook groups. Heather has become famous for her Wiggly Wigglers podcasts, which draw up to 20,000 listeners per month. So the site features in the generic search on Google and she uses Google AdWords to bring more customers to the site.

Heather describes her use of Google AdWords as intuitive rather than analytical. 'My approach is holistic rather than measurement based.' Once she had created the information-based website, she set a daily budget for the AdWords. She has dropped all her other advertising.

'I'm sure a lot of people use Google AdWords more effectively than I do, but I care more about how people react to our information on the site. We want to attract eco-enthusiastic people to it, we don't want lots of people who don't come back to find out more.' The Google analytics tool helps her track the people that come to the site having clicked on words that are related to 'composting' and then move to do other things in the garden such as buying wild flower seed and other ecological gardening products.

Heather recognized that her business did not need to pay a high price per click for use of keywords such as 'garden', which is used by what she calls 'the big boys'. She discovered that more specific keywords such as *bokashi* deliver her more customers where the Wiggly Wigglers site can rank high in the search engine.

Heather remains passionate about helping people bring a positive and measurable impact to their surroundings, however large or small their home or garden.

You know this already, of course you do, but it's such an important concept for any business today that it's worth repeating. The internet is definitely the quickest and cheapest way to reach customers. Why? Because, as Heather discovered when she set up Wiggly Wigglers, the chances are that the vast majority of your potential customers are already online looking for you.

What used to be a medium predominantly for young people has changed so rapidly that those who don't recognize it are not just in danger of being left behind, they're already invisible. The demographics of people using the internet have, as they say in the business, caught up to mainstream. Trawling the internet at this very minute are people aged from five to eighty-five. No, let's amend that, quickly, before it's overtaken again: from three to a hundred and three. People used to buy silver spoons and napkin rings for new babies; right now somebody out there is probably busy inventing a silver cordless mouse, or marketing a mobile made up of jolly multicoloured laptops that will spin and twinkle over the cot.

The big boys and girls are already throwing money at developing an online presence. But don't let that unnerve you. A small business can still get in with only a limited investment. It won't take long to find out what's going to work for you. You can easily control how much you want to spend, and, in case you're one jump ahead already and worrying about being swamped with too many orders too quickly for your distribution systems to handle, how many customers you want to attract.

We'll get to the how and what of the process later, but this is really about the why. Why you or your business should have an internet presence, if you haven't already. Why you need to do more than set up a website. Why you need to understand the secret power of words.

Look at Google. A business that began with a simple idea; to help people find things on the internet. Now Google is not just a massive multi-billion dollar business, it's a verb. People don't search for something on the web, they Google it. The people who started Google were so successful in designing its search algorithm that it became the market leader. Although there are competitors like Yahoo, it's Google that dominates. Google is a company that understands the secret power of words.

That's important because with all those billions of websites already out there, and more mushrooming by the minute; the problem is to draw people to yours, rather than to your competitors'. Your website is your online advertisement, but it's also essential somehow to advertise your website's existence. The Google AdWords programme drives more ads than anybody else on the internet, and the beauty of it is that it's accessible to everybody, not just the big players with money to throw at advertising.

KNOWING YOUR CUSTOMERS

Let's take a look at the basics you need to use Google AdWords successfully. The very first requirement is an understanding of exactly who your customers are. It's like any business proposition: first, find out who your customers are and what they want, then provide a way for them to get it. This is the basic knowledge and understanding that from the start you have to build into any product or service and the website for it.

So, when you've figured out who your customers are, and their need, you can build a website that gives them some basic information about your product or service, and contact details so they can reach you and place an order. Once that is up and running, you can begin to drive more and more visitors to it using the targeted advertising available through Google.

The more 'niche' your product, the easier this is, for the simple reason that there'll be fewer other businesses in competition with you and it'll be easier to identify your customers. Let's suppose you are the maker or supplier of a specialist product like wider-fitting walking boots. This is, in many ways, a perfect kind of product to sell via the internet, because your customers are an identifiable community, walkers, with a specific need; wider, comfortable footwear, a need often not catered for by ordinary high street retailers.

In order to draw these people to your site, rather than anyone else's, think about all the words they might key into a search engine like Google if they're looking for your product – or indeed, that might lead them to come across it by accident and then realise that it fulfils a need of theirs exactly.

You might start with words like 'boots' and 'wide-fitting', or a phrase like 'wide feet'. You could be more general and think of themes like 'outdoor clothing' or 'footwear', but you'll pull in more visitors to the site if you add a few more that relate specifically to the activities you think your customers will be interested in using their boots for – 'walking', 'hiking', 'trail', 'rambler', for instance. Or perhaps you might pick up on yet more specific themes, like 'fell-walking', 'moorland', even 'camping'. For any given product or service there'll be all kinds of themes you might develop and expand, to drive traffic to your site and grow your business.

But this is leaping ahead. Let's begin with the number one requirement for doing business via the internet, your website. If you already have a website you'll be tempted to speed through this chapter, but don't completely ignore it because it explains how your website needs to reflect the AdWords you'll be using to grow your business.

THE BASICS OF WEBSITE DESIGN: AN OVERVIEW

A great deal of thought goes into the design of a good website and it doesn't need to be all-singing, all-dancing, with videos and animation and endless pop-ups. Indeed it's often the simplest sites that work the best. Think of your site as needing to be fit for purpose. What does it need to have and to do to serve the basic needs of your customers?

Go back to those hypothetical wide-fitting walking boots. You'll need a website that gives your customers some information about them; how they're designed especially for the wider foot, possibly the different sizes and styles available, the men's version and the women's version. You'll need pictures of them, several possibly, displaying them from different angles, or in different colours and styles if these are available, pointing out any special features like their super-grip sole or their anatomically-shaped footbed. You might also consider pictures of athletic young people jumping over mountain streams wearing your boots, or posing by a dry stone wall gazing at a glorious view. Of course if you were a large company with a big budget, you could produce a clever little animation about how the bones and tendons of the foot work as a walker strides out, but that isn't necessary to sell a pair of boots to someone who's been looking all over to find a pair that will fit.

Much more important than videos or dancing boots is the information that tells them how they can buy your product. With a pair of walking boots, they might well want to try them on in a store before buying, so your website will need at the very least to provide a list of stockists and perhaps a link to their websites. On the other hand if your company sells direct to the public, they might prefer to buy the boots over the telephone, where they can talk to one of your friendly sales team, or by post, or via the site itself, in which case you might want to include information not only on how they purchase but also on your returns policy if the boots don't fit.

It's crucial to make sure your customers can get enough information from the site to bring them to the decision to buy, whatever method they'll use. In later chapters we'll talk more about how to bring them to your website in ever-increasing numbers, but for now this chapter will help you understand what's needed on your website if you're using Google AdWords. There's more information about website design in the Appendix.

What's in a name?

One of the first things to consider when planning a website that's going to make the best use of Google AdWords is your domain name, which will be part of your web address or, to give it the technical term, URL – Universal Resource Locator.

There are two possible approaches to choosing a name. You could be simply descriptive, for example, handlebars.co.uk or bikerepairgenius.com. For instance, if you're hoping to achieve success as a manufacturer or supplier of walking boots for those with wide feet, it would make obvious sense for your website address to be www.widewalkingboots.co.uk or, if you are a chiropractor living in West Hampstead, to advertise yourself as www.westhampsteadchiropractic.net.

Many of the good names have already been taken, especially if you're in a business where there are likely to be many similar traders or practitioners. So you may have to persevere and come up with something more unusual but still, ideally, descriptive of you and your business. Heather did exactly that when she choose the Wiggly Wigglers name for her business. The more adjectives you add to the name – supremelycomfortableboots.co.uk – the more likely you are to succeed in finding a name that hasn't yet been taken. Or you might find that widewalkingboots.com has been taken, but if you use dashes creatively, such as 'widewalking-boots', you might still be able to give yourself a website address close to the original thought. Bear in mind though, that as many customers as you might poach from the other, similarly named site, you could lose even more of your own who forget the dash when they type in your address.

Alternatively you could take a creative approach and pick a name that's memorable, though it doesn't necessarily have a relevant meaning or anything at all to do with your product. Apple.com is a great example of this, and has sparked many imitators. In theory, the more obscure the name, the less likely it is to be taken. Be warned, though, that many have trodden this path before you and however clever you think you are in picking an obscure, erudite name, someone else will already have snapped up many of the most evocative.

For small companies starting out, who don't yet have a brand name, the most sensible approach is to go for the first kind of domain name, something that's helpfully descriptive of your product or service. It makes your website much easier to find and more memorable. Don't assume you need to make your domain name the same as your business name. People won't necessarily remember that it's Mark Smith and Sons who manufacture or supply 'supremely comfortable walking boots', but if you pick a good domain name that contains a description of your product they'll still be able to find their way back to the Mark Smith and Sons website. The place for finding names and buying the one you want is through one of the many domain name hosting companies. If you visit one of their websites, you'll find the tools to check whether the name you want is available. If it is, you can then buy the right to use that name for a year or more, at a cost of only a few pounds. At the end of the year you'll be asked if you want to renew the domain name. As the cost is rarely more than eight or ten pounds a year, it's often worth hanging on to a good domain name even if the business that uses that name has temporarily gone on the back burner.

Dot.co.uk or dot.com?

Both these suffixes, the bit that goes at the end of your URL or web address, indicate the site is going to be primarily in English, though in theory you could build the site in any language you like. So if you choose one of these, the majority of the people who find your site will be English-speaking.

Dot.com used to be the preferred suffix for businesses because it was among the first to exist, thus suggesting you'd been trading on the web from the early days. Now, though, there are plenty of suffixes to choose from. Some carry more specialist meanings: dot.org suggests non-profit-making organizations like charities, dot.tv TV companies, dot.edu schools, dot.ac.uk British universities. Less specifically, you might also consider dot.info and dot.net.

So if someone has pipped you to the post with widewalkingboots.com, there may be nothing to stop you bagging widewalkingboots.co.uk or widewalkingboots.net. However, remember again that this could lose you as many visitors as you poach from your competitor, so what's the point? Besides, most people, when choosing a domain name, will at the same time buy up a number of obviously similar ones, including most of the obvious suffixes. The expense is minimal and it's well worth doing to save confusion between your product and someone else's site. Indeed, you can buy up as many names as you want and have them all direct people to the same webpage, but clearly you could waste a lot of money if you try to cover every possible permutation. It might be wiser to wait until you're a multi-million pound global enterprise before you start buying up too many names. For the moment, focus on getting the main website name and URL up and working well.

Choosing the right host company

Domain name hosting companies do more than sell you a name. They also provide you with web space, and thus 'host' your site. So make sure you pick a reliable and reputable company when you start the process of setting up your web address.

There are plenty of tiny web hosts that come and go, but you want a bigger company with staying power and enough customers to be sure it's reputable. Choose a company that's been in business for several years at least. If possible, look for recommendations from anyone you know who has a website.

Most of your communications with them will be via e-mail and the web, but once you're a paying customer there may be telephone support too. The more you pay, the better technical support you'll get; if you're using their least expensive version to set up a website from templates, don't expect much hand-holding.

If you decide at some point to change to a different domain name hosting company, you should still be able to take your domain name with you. It's much the same as switching your phone provider but keeping your number; there'll usually be a small additional charge.

One step at a time

It's not a bad idea to use a template to design your website to start off with. If you want more information about how to do it yourself, you'll find it in the Appendix at the end of this book. When you first set up a website, you're really experimenting to see how it could work for you. Of course you want to give it a good enough shot that it won't turn out an unmitigated disaster and put you off online advertising for life, but your first website is often a case of taking the temperature of the water before you plunge right in and thoroughly immerse yourself. What you're after is a sense of how advertising online could help your business. This isn't like any other form of marketing. In traditional forms of advertising, let's say print or broadcasting, costs are high, you buy your slot and you get one shot, so it's vital to get it right first time. But online you can afford to proceed step by step. You can try new things, without finding yourself locked in. Getting a website up quickly, and then improving on it later, is a better and cheaper way of testing the market than spending ages mulling over different designs and trying to make your site 100 per cent perfect straight out of the gate.

So, returning to those wider-fitting walking boots, you're not an experienced footwear designer or manufacturer but someone who has wide feet themselves, loves walking, but couldn't find anything to fit. On a walking holiday in the Apennines, you fell into step with a big-footed American who noticed you hobbling and told you about his mother's uncle Silvio, who has a small family firm near Naples making shoes to traditional principles. He'll custom-make you a pair of boots. Silvio's boots turn out to be so comfortable and so surprisingly cheap that you realize it would be possible to enlist his help in designing a wider-fitting walking boot for others like you. You think you've spotted a gap in the market but this is the first time you've dipped your toe, so to speak, in the shoe business. Will it work? Are there really enough people out there with wide feet who'll pay the premium for Silvio's heavenly boots? You've commissioned a limited, prototype line from him and you want to see if your idea will work. Now you're considering a basic website, to see how many customers you can attract online with a trial marketing of the boots.

At this early stage, all you'll need is a site consisting of two pages. The first page is the hook to interest the customer in the product and consists of a short description of what the product is, in words and pictures. Clearly, a picture of Silvio's supremely comfortable walking boots is essential, but should you be advertising a service rather than a product, you'll still need to include a picture or pictures, because when they're thinking about buying something, people often respond better to a visual stimulus. So even if you are, say, a chiropractor advertising your practice, make sure on your page there's a picture of a human spine, or a client being treated on your table.

The second page will be the call to action. This could include more detail of your product, or an order form. It could have an e-mail click-through that lets your client contact you simply by clicking on the e-mail address to bring up a pop-up where they can write their message and send it directly to you. This, and all sorts of other possibilities, can be incorporated in your site via a template.

The homepage: your shop window

The homepage is usually the first page that visitors to your site will see, and the place from where they start their journey through your products and services to a possible purchase. It's the page they reach when they tap in your web address, and so it's the most important piece of the web design. It has to create a good impression and make people want to go further into the site to learn more about you and your product. If you have a larger, more complex site consisting of several pages, the homepage is not so much a doorway in, as a hallway which will contain many different doors visitors can enter depending on what they're looking for. One of those doorways, very likely marked **Contact us**, should take visitors to a way of making contact, via e-mail, telephone or your postal address.

The hallway, just like the hallway in a home or in an office building, has to be sufficiently attractive to entice visitors in and to make them want to travel further through the site. If it feels dingy and cramped, people will back away and go somewhere else. The design and décor of that 'hallway' can say a lot about you and your business, so it's worth spending some time thinking about how to make it look attractive to your customers. Your options may be more limited if you're working from templates, but there'll still be some choice. Colours can be eye-catching, but make sure they're also harmonious. Your favourite colours may be purple and green, but will they appeal to the kind of people you want to attract as customers? Keep the text simple and large enough to read easily, especially if you're aiming for older customers whose eyesight may not be so good.

When you've finished it, before you go live with the site, 'publishing' it on the internet, show it to people you know and you trust to be honest in their responses. Being willing to listen to other people's suggestions about the look and feel of the site produces the best result.

Then, when you're satisfied with the initial design and content, hit the 'publish' button and wait for a response from customers.

You can be too successful!

As your website creates more traffic, more people visiting it, it may be worth thinking about spending more money on it. This isn't only a question of giving it a more professional look. It's also about making sure it doesn't crash under the numbers of people trying to access it all at once. That's a good problem to have, because it should mean you're doing very good business and you can afford an upgrade!

A thousand people a day visiting your site sounds a lot, and could be very exciting for your business. But most servers should be able to cope easily with those numbers. But half a million a day, and there'll definitely be a problem.

And how will all those people have found out about your site. The next chapter will tell you all.

TOP TIPS

 AdWords offers a level playing field. It allows anyone to compete with larger companies having more financial muscle, particularly if you're offering a niche product.

 If you just want to test the market you can use a template and create a web page rather than an entire website.

 Once you've decided on your product or service, identify exactly your customers and their needs. Your website should simply serve the needs of your customers.

 Choose the name of your website carefully. Ideally, especially with a new business, it's worth settling on a name that's helpfully descriptive of the product or service you're offering.

 Make sure your website offers visitors clear and easy details of how to buy your product. This is very important!

 Make sure you choose a reputable hosting company for your website.

Question

What's in a name?

Action

The name you give your website is an important business decision. One of the first things to consider when planning a website that is going to make the best use of Google AdWords is your URL – Universal Resource Locator – which is going to help your customers find your product. So you need to decide if you are going to describe your product in the name of your website, or if you want to invent a memorable name that can never be forgotten.

CHAPTER 3
GOOGLE AND THE SECRET NEED

Google's search engine started officially in 1998. Yahoo and AltaVista were already well established leaders in the field, but within just five years Google had overtaken them because its first page of results was much closer to what the average person was looking for. This strength of relevance to the search words is why Google AdWords outshines its competitors.

This chapter explains why the Google search engine is an excellent tool for advertising your product or service. We'll discuss:

- how Google's 'PageRank' system works;

- how Google makes AdWords work and why it's so successful;

- why AdWords is more effective than just about any other kind of advertising;

- how and why Google's approach favours the customer above all else.

Enviro-light – www.enviro-light.co.uk

Liam Darch-Wood started an entirely new business model of retailing based on the Google search engine. Liam's story begins with a problem in the kitchen. He's a very keen cook and likes to try Italian-inspired food that he prepares for his wife Vikki while the left overs are gobbled up by his lovely cocker spaniel, Fudge. The problem isn't the cooking but the light bulbs in the kitchen. He told me:

> We have a lighting rack with $4 \times$ MR16 spotlights on; they seem to go all the time and I would hazard a guess at around 14 or 15 a year. I think it might be grease from the cooking that makes them blow. I used to have to physically take the blown bulb to B&Q to get exactly what I wanted and you can only buy them in packs of 2.

Liam's search for light bulbs was the inspiration for his website Enviro-light.co.uk where he offers savings by buying light bulbs in packs of 4, 10s and 20s. Liam understands retail because he left school halfway through his A levels to work for Morrison's supermarkets. He became their youngest ever department manager at 20 and his store in Derby was also in the top ten stores in terms of turnover. But his real business interest is in search engine sales, and Enviro-light.co.uk is part of his company, TDW Commerce, which he plans to become an empire of e-commerce stores, all driven by search engines. Enviro-light.co.uk is the first product of this project with Caravan & Camping equipment the next in the pipeline. Liam is convinced that Google Adwords creates an entirely new business model of retailing, based on the Google search engine.

He's sympathetic to the problems of the traditional retailers. 'If you open a shop you have to pay rent on the space and you have to stock the whole shop with every single item.' As a customer looking for light bulbs for his kitchen, he walked round the DIY stores looking at their racks and racks of light bulbs, feeling frustrated that the bulb he was looking for wasn't available. He says:

in a shop you can't display every item and therefore a customer will think you don't actually sell it and there are literally tens of thousands of different bulbs that you can buy. You probably buy a light fitting and you never really know what bulb goes in it until you've got it home and realise that you can't get bulbs for it.

So Liam's site specializes in the more difficult to obtain bulbs such as those needed for security or decorative lighting. Liam knows his customers suddenly discover they need a specialist bulb and want to find it quickly.

When he began the business Liam set a clear budget of the price of a pair of shoes a day and has been happy with the return. He's used AdWords to advertise one section of lighting at a time, starting with halogen lights. This allowed the business to keep customers focused in one area, and build up stock in that particular section before moving to a new lighting area. So the company uses AdWords to build knowledge of the customer and stock at the same time.

But how do you describe a light bulb? It's more difficult than you might first think. For example, a very small halogen capsule light bulb caused him problems. Liam described how on the box and in the catalogue the light was described as 'capsule' and he assumed that would be the word customers would use in their online search. He was wrong. He used as many different varieties of how people might describe the bulb, waited a week, then analysed the data.

We tried 'halogen capsule' or 'halogen capsules', 'capsule lamps', 'capsule lamp', and there wasn't a lot of traffic for something that should be selling quite well, so then we tried describing the light by the name of the fitting – 'G4 bulbs' and 'G4 halogen bulbs' and immediately the traffic patterns changed dramatically.

At this point Liam rewrote his advert, so instead of saying 'We sell halogen capsules', it said 'We sell G4 bulbs'. What Liam discovered was that to sell the capsule light bulb he needed Google AdWords 'G4 bulb' or 'G4 halogen bulb'.

Liam's other key learning is the importance of uniformity between the keyword searched for, the advert delivered, and what is viewed on the website. When he discovered that G4 halogen bulbs and G4 bulbs were the two most popular search words, he made sure the advert contained that particular key phrase. When customers go through to the landing page of the website, the key phrase is also prominent.

Liam uses conversion tracking that shows when a sale has been triggered by a particular advert or keyword. Through the conversion tracking, he assesses which of the landing pages was most effective over a period of time. Conversion tracking is a very simple piece of code that Liam has placed on the website pages that say 'Thank you for your order' and 'Your order has been successful'. These are the pages of his website that mean a sale has taken place. As soon as somebody gets to that page, it triggers the code, and Google can track back to what keyword and which advert they clicked on.

He did this using the Conversion Tracking button on the website and clicking on 'is this is a sale or an enquiry or a lead'. He said, 'you literally press a button and it generates a code for you, five lines of java script. I sent it to my web developer and he just popped it in the page. It only takes a couple of minutes to put up and only needs to be done once.' Now Liam can see how many clicks he's had and the cost per conversion, all on one screen. Your conversion code is available within your AdWords account, under the tools section. If you have access to your website html, you copy and paste the code into your html, just above the closing tag towards the end of the page.

So what was the most difficult part in setting up the business? Nothing to do with the AdWords! It was packaging. 'The most difficult thing for me was just the logistics of posting out a light bulb and how I would deal with that, not how I was going to get the business that was out there.'

HOW GOOGLE RANKS PAGES

Google was founded by Larry Page and Sergey Brin while they were students at Stanford University. Their mission was 'to organize the world's information and make it universally accessible and useful'. They thought they had a better angle on how searching could work. Their key insight was that the best way to decide whether a page is relevant, the most appropriate one to meet the search you're typing in, is by how many other people link to it. They worked on the simple premise that if your website has a lot of people linking to it from other web pages it's pretty likely that it has good stuff on it. If other people are telling the world that they think your page is worth reading by putting a link on their page to yours, it's a good way of measuring how useful the information on the page might be. Page and Brin came up with a concept that they called 'PageRank', which evaluates the quality and appropriateness of any web page based on how many other people link to it.

PageRank is an algorithm, a mathematical process that, following a search, determines which page shows up first, second, third and so on. Google describes it as interpreting 'a link from Page A to Page B as a vote by Page A for Page B'. In other words, a PageRank comes from 'balloting' all the pages on the World Wide Web about how important a particular page is. A page with a higher PageRank is considered to be more important and is more likely to be listed above a page with a lower PageRank.

However, Google doesn't just look at the sheer number of links a page receives. It also analyses the page casting the vote, so that votes cast by higher ranking pages count for more and help to make other pages 'important'. There are many other factors that influence PageRank but Google keeps a lot of them under wraps. It's completely automated so there are no humans involved in the ranking mechanism.

Google uses a web crawler, also known as a spider, which it calls Googlebot, to find and fetch web pages that are stored in Google's vast database. Googlebot consists of many computers requesting and fetching thousands of different pages simultaneously. These pages are scanned for hyperlinks which provide new documents to be fetched and stored in the same way. All the words, except for common words such as the, is, or, on these pages are indexed so that when a search is entered the search words can be located in the enormous index and pages containing those words identified. That's when PageRank comes in to rank the pages in order of relevance. One of the things that helped Google get so big is that it's very good at building cheap, efficient computers, and it runs a network of thousands of them so it can carry out very fast data processing. If you want to know more about this have a look at www.Googleguide.com/Google_works.html, an online tutorial not affiliated to Google itself.

There were a handful of other search engines before Google arrived on the scene. Yahoo was one of the first;

others included AltaVista, Infoseek and Excite. But the Google algorithm proved so superior that many search engines disappeared and those that remained have been overshadowed by Google as it grew to its current gargantuan size. This helps you and me because we can focus all our energies on the one search engine since it's so far ahead of its competitors. What's more; Google continually improves its search. The latest round of improvements are called 'caffeine', so with confidence we can expect a faster service.

GOOGLE'S NEXT BIG IDEA

Originally, Google's big idea was about searching, not advertising; it was simply a search engine. But the next big revolution in Google happened in 2000 when it introduced AdWords, which allowed advertisers to create text ads for placement on the Google search engine. Google wasn't the first company to think about advertising in this way. GoTo, which later changed its name to Overture and is now part of Yahoo, was the first to successfully provide a pay-per-click (PPC) search service. For this kind of service, advertisers typically only pay their host when their ad is clicked. Overture was a straight auction model. Advertisers decided the maximum amount they were prepared to pay for an ad spot and the automated auction was triggered whenever a visitor clicked on the ad. The advertiser with the highest bid got the best position of the ad on the search results page.

On a Google search results page there are typically ten ads on the right-hand side of the page, headed Sponsored Links. Sometimes they also appear along the top of the page. Naturally, the lower your ad is down that page, the less likely it is to be clicked. And if you are eleventh, and on the second page, then you might as well be wearing a cloak of invisibility. But don't worry, by reading this book you'll find out exactly how to keep your ad right near the top of the list.

Google could see that Overture was working quite successfully but because Google puts great stock in employing a lot of very smart engineers, computer scientists and similar big-brained eggheads, it soon found ways to improve on the model.

The main improvement is that the position of your ad is based not just on how much you pay, but also on how well your ad performs.

If you have an ad that's very relevant and performs very, very well Google will give you a boost in your ranking for the same amount of money. As you know from Liam's experience, if you have one ad saying 'converse bulb' versus another saying 'G4 halogen bulb', the ad that's more appealing is the one that fits what's being searched for and gets clicked on more often, so it'll get an advantage.

Google kept the secret of this clever system under wraps and no one ever knew exactly whether they would get top spot or not. But later in this book we are going to reveal that secret, show you how to grab that top ranking and demonstrate how you can produce a low-cost, high-performance advertisement for your business.

That's what this book is all about; the ads and how they perform. So keep on reading.

The reason why AdWords are so effective compared with other advertising (they actually perform between two and ten times better) is because when someone is actively searching for something like a new car they're already in the mood to buy. If you can put a relevant ad in front of that person then you're much more likely to make a sale.

Google spotted that the search was a very strong indication of desire to purchase and that advertisements can fulfil the need of the searcher. All other advertising media, like newspapers, magazines, television, are mass market. Everybody will see a television ad for a light bulb whether they're looking to buy one or not. If you're an advertiser, you're wasting money on the 99.99 per cent of people who aren't in the market for light bulbs. If you advertise on Google, though, the only people who will see your ad for a light bulb are those who are actually interested in purchasing one, which means more effective advertising with greater efficiency.

You might get closer to your purchaser if you advertise your light bulbs in a home improvements magazine or on a TV channel devoted to home makeover shows, but again those readers or viewers aren't necessarily looking to buy light bulbs, especially as many readers and viewers of even these specialist media don't actually do any home improvements; they just find the programme relaxing or they fancy the presenter. Most of the audience probably already have the light bulbs they want or perhaps they're simply not in the mood to buy when they're browsing a magazine or watching television. Working with a specific genre media is good, but it's still not the same as an internet search when someone is actively looking. It's the 'active' versus 'passive' that makes the difference. The person doing a search is leaning forward, not sitting back.

If you're actively searching for a light bulb for your new and unusual light fitting, your behaviour is going to be different from when you're browsing a magazine and happen to see a halogen bulb ad. Searching for a product online is especially effective if you've a clear idea of what you want because the advertisements are going to be targeted directly towards your needs.

Google's massive computing power gives it a genuine advantage over competitors, because it can search, analyse the AdWords, and reveal the results at such a tremendous speed.

THE MORE EFFECTIVE THE AD, THE LESS IT COSTS

Google's motto is 'don't do evil'. Unlike the auction of advertisements, which favours those with more money and is aimed at quickly generating a lot of income for the search provider, Google wants to make sure that people can find the information they're looking for as easily as possible and to provide the most satisfying experience for all the people who use its website.

The ads that Google runs alongside the search results are rated on how well they perform. If the ad is not performing well, which means it's not being clicked on, it probably indicates it's not very relevant to the search that person was doing, Google will correspondingly drop the ad down the page and finally stop showing it. In this way, your experience of searching online for halogen bulbs will be better because if someone has written a poor or irrelevant ad, Google won't even show it to you. It wants to make your search experience as helpful as possible.

It may be making billions of dollars, but Google is still very customer-orientated. In fact, you might even say that it's making those billions because it focuses on the customer. By reading this book and being customer-orientated yourself, you can make money as well.

Google now has an 80 per cent market share of online advertising, but there are other search engines you might consider. In the Appendix to this book, we show you how

Yahoo and Bing, two similar search engines, work. There are different methods for building your ads in each and there are differences, for example, on how many words you are allowed to use in your ad.

Google's market capitalization is now over $100 billion, with more than $20 billion annual revenue. And it's still growing. So we know that AdWords really works. OK, how do you make it work for you?

It's actually easy. Anybody can do it. To use Google AdWords you don't have to work for a top advertising agency. You can do it at home and there's no big mystery to it. In the next chapter, I'm going to show you how.

And the big ideas keep on coming: AdSense

Google AdSense is a Google programme based on content rather than on search. Website owners who sign up for AdSense can display Google ads on their websites and receive money for any clicks on the ads. So now you're asking, 'Could I make money from my website if I sign up for AdSense?' The answer's yes, and although this book really concentrates on your advertising, we've added a section in the Appendix that explains how you can profit from AdSense.

TOP TIPS

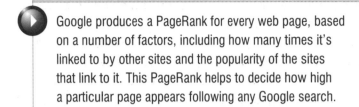 Google produces a PageRank for every web page, based on a number of factors, including how many times it's linked to by other sites and the popularity of the sites that link to it. This PageRank helps to decide how high a particular page appears following any Google search.

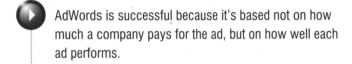 AdWords is successful because it's based not on how much a company pays for the ad, but on how well each ad performs.

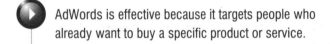 AdWords is effective because it targets people who already want to buy a specific product or service.

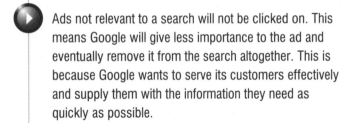 Ads not relevant to a search will not be clicked on. This means Google will give less importance to the ad and eventually remove it from the search altogether. This is because Google wants to serve its customers effectively and supply them with the information they need as quickly as possible.

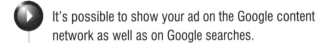 It's possible to show your ad on the Google content network as well as on Google searches.

Question

Do you understand algorithms?

Action

Luckily you don't need to understand algorithms! They are part of the back office element of Google AdWords. All you need to know is that there is a mathematical process that works out which page shows up first when someone searches for a word in the Google search engine. You want your website to be high in the search results, and the more successful your site becomes the more likely it is to get to the top of the page in the automated search engine. The more people who visit and click through from your advertisement then the higher your website will be in the page ranking.

CHAPTER 4
THE SECRET BEHIND PAY-PER-CLICK ADVERTISING

If you want to sell things online you need to make sure your advertisement is relevant to the person searching for information about the subject. This chapter will discuss how to go about ensuring your ad is at the top of the search results page.

It'll explain:

- how to make the right people click on your ad;

- how to start choosing the best keywords for your site;

- how to target your ads effectively at the people most likely to become paying customers.

Choosing the right words and getting the best value from pay-per-click on the Anna Brooks website

Annabrooks.com is a website that sells dresses to what they call 'plus size' ladies who want to buy formal wear. It's a site for women who need a smart dress for a special occasion; the marriage of their son or daughter, a black tie dinner, an important do at work, for example.

The website owner is Vicky Prezeau. She uses Google AdWords to grow this niche business, which she runs at present from home but plans to expand, because 'plus size' is a growing market, particularly in the US.

Her first problem was the name of the site. Her URL 'annabrooks.com' is not related to plus size dresses, so she relies on a high 'quality score' from Google in order to get her website high in the search engine. She followed the list of Google's instructions to get a high score when she developed the website:

1 The overall layout and functionality must be simple and attractive.

2 It must be both easy to navigate and informative.

3 It must keep the user experience in mind.

Here are some ways in which to ensure your website meets those criteria:

● Place important information and images on the top left, where the eye naturally goes first.

● Help people get what they want in a maximum of three clicks.

● Cut out popups and popunders.

● Create a simple process for users to complete transactions.

Google uses metatags to check that the site has information on it that is relevant to Vicky's keywords, so the position that she ranks in Google is not just because of how much she paid for the ad but because the site is relevant to the search.

Vicky's first tip is to make sure your site is built really well before you begin advertising.

When she started her AdWord sales campaign she considered using the most obvious word that would be searched for: 'dresses'. Such a broad keyword would deliver millions of clicks with AdWords, but the dresses Vicky sells are all a particular kind of style, conservative, traditional, 'mother of the bride' garments. Vicky calculated that only a small percentage of the women who type 'dresses' into Google will be plus size women looking for formal wear.

So the AdWords she's used instead are much more specific: 'Blue, lacy, mother of the bride, out-size dress' gives her the top place in the search and when the user clicks to her website she has made a sale in the process.

She told me:

> I only want somebody to see my site if they're interested in plus size formal wear. I don't care about anybody else because they're not going to buy anything and that means I'll have paid for a click but I don't get any money back. So even if I had millions of dollars to spend I still wouldn't want to bid on the word 'dresses' because the chances are that I'd burn through a huge amount of cash and would never make money on that word.

Exact phrase versus broad match

Vicky's second tip is for selling in a niche market. She uses phrase matching by putting her keyword phrase between quotation marks. That ensures the person who sees your ad has searched within their search words for the exact words they would buy a dress, but of course there's a downside, if she hadn't used quotation marks she'd have had a 'broad' match which would have given her more traffic to her site. For plus size dresses Vicky thinks a broad match is a high risk strategy and she says it will 'burn through a lot of money' for a small return.

Writing the ad and using groups

Vicky is selling both mother of the bride dresses and holiday party dresses for plus size women. So she needs different ads targeted for the different prospects. With Google, the ad has to be relevant to the keywords, so she groups her keywords and writes ads that are relevant for that group of keywords. She creates between three and five different advertisements for a particular group of keywords and then loads them all up into Google and sees which ones generate the most clicks. The popular ads are then served more frequently.

Her third tip is to check which ads make you the most money. This is obvious, but beginners often forget that Google is only looking at clicks; that's how it makes its money. It's not looking at sales on your site. You could write an ad that's great for generating clicks but terrible for generating sales. And Google just chooses the one that generates clicks. You need to run the ad that generates sales, such as 'Dress size 30 blue lacy mother of the bride'.

She's found that specific phrases create more sales because there aren't that many people searching on AdWords for a size 30 blue lacy mother of the bride dress. The people that do click on this specific ad are very likely to buy the product.

Vicky's final tip is that specific is cheaper as you only have to pay Google when someone clicks on your ad. Vicky does not have to buy many clicks to keep her business healthy and when she does pay Google for a click, at least the chances are that it will have led to a sale.

If your advertisement is relevant, Google will charge you less for clicks and your customers will also reward you by buying what you have to sell. If your ads aren't relevant then Google is not the right place for you to advertise. The Google network reaches more than 80 per cent of internet users worldwide. If your ad gets clicked, it's what people are searching for and you have reached the right ones. If your ad isn't clicked, it isn't good enough so you will pay more and get a lower place on the page. The best advice then is to drop the ad altogether, it's a dead duck. The higher your click-through rate, the more people who see your ad and click on it, the less you have to pay for the position you want. This is the basic rule to remember.

MAKING THE RIGHT PEOPLE CLICK ON YOUR AD

Imagine that, like Vicky, you're selling dresses. Say you've bid to pay Google the price of a cup of tea for every person who clicks over to your website. You don't want time-wasters visiting your site because you'll still have to pay that cup of tea price for every one of them, while not getting any sales. On the other hand, you need to have an attractive advertisement so that genuine potential customers come to your website, not to your competitors who are also selling dresses. To achieve this you have to use the right words in your headline.

A good example of an ad headline: 'Average price plus size dress'

This is a specific headline. It tells you what you are going to get and what the price is.

A bad example: 'Free postage on dresses'

This headline is too attractive. It doesn't 'pre-qualify' your click. People looking for freebies just see the word free and click to see further details. You've paid for them to reach you, but they are a poor prospect because they're mainly motivated by the idea of something free. They aren't going to buy one of your plus size dresses.

When you do a search on Google, the search engine results page is the page that comes back with all the results of that search. The main elements on the results page are the natural results shown on the main part of the page; but along the right-hand side, and sometimes across the top, is a list of sponsored links. And those sponsored links are the AdWords that the advertisers are buying. So if you type in 'plus size dress', you're going to get ten sponsored links on the right, or occasionally, at the top. If there's a very relevant result Google will give it top spot and display it in a different colour.

Google matches the words that someone types into the search to the words that will make your ad appear. These words don't actually have to appear in your ad, but you will have decided which words should trigger the advertisement to appear. As an example, your ad might be 'blue dress average price', but some of the words you've chosen to make your ad show are 'plus size'.

When Mrs On-a-Diet searches for 'plus size', the results are displayed on the results page, with ten sponsored links at the side of the page. If your website 'plussizedresses' is one of these ads and Mrs On-a-Diet clicks through to your website, it is at that point that a potential lead has shown an interest and you, the advertiser, will pay a fee for that click depending on what you bid in the auction. You pay Google because each click demonstrates that someone has shown some interest in your ad.

When Mrs On-a-Diet clicks on your ad it should take her directly to the relevant page of your website which will tell her more about the product. With any luck she'll place an order. Then you make money and everybody's happy.

So the first thing to do to get your ad to the top of the list of sponsored links is to make sure that your advertisement is relevant.

MAKING SURE YOUR WEBSITE TURNS SEARCHERS INTO PURCHASERS

Your first step is to come up with a list of words that people might type in when they're searching to buy a plus size dress. Google calls these words 'keywords', and although there are tools within Google to help you choose these, understanding your own business is the most important element of this process. The words you select as keywords are also words that you've probably included already on your website. Things like 'large size', 'extra large', 'plus size', 'mother of the bride', in fact all the different words that relate to the dresses and to buying a plus size dress for a special occasion. Make a list of all of those keywords and put them into your account.

Google has strict rules about these words and if you break them they'll disallow your ads. For example, you can't use all capital letters, you can't have more than one exclamation mark(!), and you can't use somebody else's brand name unless you're actually selling that brand or have some association with it. So you can't say 'better than Evans outsize clothes', or 'more choice than Harrods', because you're not associated with those brands. This goes back to Google's motto, 'don't do evil'. Google wants the page to be as useful as possible to the customers, the people who are doing the search, and when you start using excessive punctuation and lots of shouty capitals it becomes harder to read. So you have to be careful not to break their rules.

You usually have only a few seconds to get someone's attention when they are on a page so people have to understand your message very quickly. You can't get very complicated because Google only allows you 25 characters for the headline and 35 for the actual ad, really only a few words, so simplicity and clarity is vital.

Let's take the example of health insurance, which in the USA is quite expensive and is price-sensitive. Headlines such as 'compare health plan prices, apply online and save', or 'get affordable health insurance', are all relevant to the buyers. More importantly, they also attract people who are ready to buy. Someone just looking around as part of a school research project would type in 'health insurance' or 'health insurance plans' in their search. But someone actually looking to buy would type in 'affordable insurance', which is more specific. The more accurate the search words, the more likely it is that the person is in buying mode. This is what Vicky did when she used the words 'mother of the bride plus size dress' and this is the secret of keywords.

Put as many relevant keywords as possible into your account and test them to see which ones work. AdWords has a facility to track your words and over time this enables you to find out which of them are making you the most money. Then, you can spend more on the most effective keywords and delete those with the fewest clicks.

You can use negative keywords to make sure that a casual browser or someone looking for a freebie won't see your ad. An example that relates to health insurance would be 'pet' or 'dog', because you only sell human health insurance so you don't want your ad to show when the searcher types 'dog health insurance'.

Before we move on, there are two common mistakes I want to warn you about. The first is to omit important keywords from the advert wording. Not only is this potentially a missed sales opportunity, it also means the campaign misses easy brownie points with Google and may lose its top position. If your business is specific to one area or locality, the name of the place will be one of your keywords.

The second error is not taking advantage of the local traffic to your site. Of course the internet is a global phenomenon, but exciting as it may be to attract visitors from Korea or Australia to your site, it may not be strictly relevant if yours happens to be a man-with-a-van business based in Yorkshire.

Fortunately, Google offers you tools to help you localize your web ads, enabling you to target them so that they only attract local traffic. You can use their 'Geotargeting' for countries, regions and cities. You can also explain on the website itself if there are any location issues. This is all part of good content design for your website, which in turn comes from knowing which customers you want to attract.

TOP TIPS

Ensure your keywords relate to your website. If Google decides that your keywords are not relevant to your website then it won't display them.

Google highlights in bold the searched keywords in the ad. Keywords highlighted in bold help to catch a person's attention, so an ad with the keyword in the headline will usually perform better than one without.

Have one theme or group of keywords called an Ad Group for each ad.

Although it's tempting to squash as many keywords as possible into the account, restrict yourself to phrases which really reflect the nature of your business. Go through your website and pick out the most relevant terms.

The secret of Google AdWords is relevance and quality.

When writing your ads, make sure you don't flout Google's rules, so no excessive exclamation marks or UNNECESSARY capital letters!!

The more accurate the search words typed into Google, the more likely a person is to be in buying mode. Put yourself in the frame of mind of your potential customers and try specifically to match their possible searches.

Relevance and accuracy can save you money. The more people who see your ad and click on it, the less you have to pay for the position you want for your ad, because Google rewards popular, relevant ads.

 Use the AdWords facility that allows you to track which of your keywords have been most successful and which have resulted in actual sales. Delete the least successful ads.

 If you're running a local business, Google can help make sure your ad only reaches local people.

 You can use an AdWords setting that means your ad will only be seen if someone searches for the exact words you've written. But although this means you maximize the chances of clicks-through resulting in sales, you also run the risk of missing out on potential customers who type in a slightly different search.

CASE STUDY

Empire Farm selling geese at Xmas

Empire Farm is a 100 acre organic farm on the edge of the Blackmore Vale, just south of Wincanton in Somerset. For the past five years the farmers, Sally and Adrian Morgan, have been raising organic geese, ducks, chickens, turkeys, sheep and pigs, mostly traditional and rare breeds. The products available vary during the year, and meat from the animals can be purchased from the online shop. Sally Morgan has used Google AdWords to sell organic geese in the run up to Christmas.

Sally and Adrian are what they call 'new farmers'. Sally is a teacher and runs courses on how to be a smallholder or poultry keeper. She spends her life between managing the farm office, looking after the animals and running the courses; and then towards the end of the year she sells organic geese for the Christmas market.

The business started from nothing and by her second Christmas at the farm she had 150 geese to sell and no experience of direct marketing. She began by advertising in the powerful tool because 'having typed out my address and my short sentence, we had three e-mails waiting for us the next morning'.

The geese are plucked and dressed on the farm and then sent by mail to the customer. Sally quickly found the keywords that worked. 'We found them so successful I've had little need to change them too much.' But she also keeps a close eye on her competitors. She recognizes that 'there's not a huge amount of competition in the market place. So getting our position on the page is not too difficult for us, particularly if we mention the word "organic".'

She spends about a bit more than the price of a pair of shoes a week on words such as 'Empire Farm goose', 'Luxury organic goose for Christmas' and 'organic, limited supplies'. So far the words 'luxury organic goose for Christmas, limited numbers' has achieved the most hits, but Wincanton is not an affluent area of Somerset and organic goose priced at about a third of a price of a pair of shoes a kilo was above what the local market would pay. Sally said, 'They would just laugh and say they could get a whole goose for much less. So we knew we had to look for more affluent markets beyond our home area. We looked at alternative ways of online marketing and realized that AdWords was a very good way of working.'

Sally thinks she's been successful because at Christmas customers are prepared to search online to get something special. Her business is niche; there are only ten or twelve people selling goose at Christmas online so she's not competing against hundreds of other pages showing organic geese for sale.

After the first couple of years selling online she noticed a reluctance among customers to pick up the phone and follow the order through:

> *I don't know whether I'm right but I feel that the person who does their searching online has got their credit card in their hand and just wants to get the job done. They don't want to have to ring and order on the phone.*

So Sally created a shopping facility on the website. She bought a readymade package for online shopping, 'it was dead easy to do. The "World Pay" at the end is taken care of by an agency, through the bank, and it's very easy to maintain.'

She has three top tips for other entrepreneurs who plan to sell online in a niche market. The first is to pay attention to the information you give on the website as well as the selling message. She thinks that people like to read about the products and she puts special effort into making sure the Empire Farm website reflects her values, friendly, approachable and organic. She aims to be more than just a shop front, in fact a place where the customer can see what's happening on the farm and what a good life the animals have had. This makes good business sense because the customer will pay more for organic geese and they can see online videos of the geese running around in the field. Her view is that with remote purchase the customers need to trust the website they're buying from, and she wants to show clearly the welfare standards on the farm.

Sally's second tip is to research competitors and see what words they're using. She says:

> *I'm quite nosy. I'll look when I'm in the browser to see which keywords they're using in their metatags. There are 3 or 4 goose competitors that I'm very keen to keep a close eye on, I'll see which keywords bring their adverts up and where they sit on the page. I want to get our*

keywords right on the website as well, so that the spiders find us without having to go through our advert, and save us some pennies.

Her final tip is to stop your adverts as soon as you've sold everything. She had sold out of geese but forgot to turn off the Google adverts. 'I suddenly realized I'd spent the value of two pairs of shoes worth of advertising because I didn't turn it off quickly enough.'

Sally is working hard to re-establish orchards at her farm so she can graze geese under the apple trees in the traditional manner. And she may even attempt some cider making. Sounds like a good combination with the geese!

Before you do anything else and before you start spending money on your ads, it's important to stop and consider exactly what kind of business you're running. From there you can start to understand who your customers might be and what they might type into a Google search. There are broadly four different kinds of online business:

1 Physical product: This is the most simple and straightforward online business. Sally Morgan had the product,150 geese ready for Christmas dinner, she just needed customers. Now she's selling educational courses to customers who'd like to keep their own poultry, so she has moved into a service industry. Amazon was one of the early pioneers of e-commerce and it originally concentrated on selling books online. But as the internet evolved, Amazon moved with the times and now you can buy anything on their site from books to music, cookery equipment, clothes, jewellery and even sex aids.

People are now much more comfortable about purchasing items online and, perhaps surprisingly, items such as shoes and clothes have become big business. Companies such as zappos.com, an American online shoe company, or Schuh.com, a UK based company you'll read about in the next case study, work hard to provide the very best customer service to encourage people to buy online. It goes without saying if you're buying any kind of clothing from the internet you can't be totally sure it will fit, so companies such as these make sure they offer very simple returns policies to give their customers total peace of mind.

2 Non-physical product: As the name suggests, these are products that don't have physical attributes. They would include insurance, for car, home, and health. A customer can search online, research all the different aspects and costs of policies for a range of companies, and then actually complete the transaction online.

3 Lead generation: This is a relatively new class of online product and it quite often deals with what are termed 'big needs', for instance buying a house or a car. With such large and important purchases, people won't want to buy without first seeing the actual product, so lead generation is a kind of 'product' that provides the sort of information that may eventually result in people physically visiting car dealerships to see a car or estate agents to view a house. Such websites are not selling products; they're providing information that could lead to the sale of a product. Car dealers in particular are willing to spend a lot of money

providing information online that will convince people to come and visit their dealership to purchase a car.

4 Physical service: If you run a small business involved, for example, in watch repairs, you're offering a service that cannot be completed online. But you might want to advertise your service online so that local people will visit your premises. This works very similarly to Yellow Pages. Someone has a broken watch; they search online and find your ad with details about your local service. You can target your local area very specifically and provide contact information that will result in enquiries to your business, whether it's a watch repair shop, a hairdresser or a dry cleaning service.

'Hard disk recovery services' represent one of the most expensive clicks on AdWords for this kind of business. People will search these kinds of keywords if their computer has crashed and they're absolutely desperate to get it fixed and retrieve their valuable data. The cost for these clicks is high, as much as two cups of coffee in the US, simply because anyone clicking on that link is almost definitely going to become a paying customer.

Using your product as a test case

If you're setting up a new business or perhaps seeking to expand your existing one, you might want to discover how big your potential market is before you commit too much money, especially if your idea needs significant investment to get it moving. Understandably, you'd like a reasonable idea of your chances of success.

Let's go back to our wide-fitting boots case study example. A quick and cost-effective way of taking the pulse of the sort of demand there might be for a shoe shop in your area is to set up a simple, one-page website that contains the basic details about your business. Then set up an AdWords account to advertise it. The volume of clicks over perhaps a three- or four-week period would tell you a lot about whether there's an opportunity there or not. If only one person visited your site in that time you might decide it's not a good investment. But if a few dozen or more reached your landing page, then you're in business! Easy. A quick and simple way of testing the water without having to part with a lot of cash. Try it.

Enticing your customers

Let's say you've done your AdWords market research. You've decided your new shoe repair business is a good prospect and you name your new venture, 'Fancy Footwork' The immodiate problem here Is that your new 'brand' is not known by anybody. There is no chance that anyone is going to type 'Fancy Footwork Shoes Repair' into a Google search, unless your Mum wants to see your website.

So, instead of using the name of your business in your ads, you need to focus on the problem you're solving, fixing broken shoes, rather than the name of your service.

Let's use another example and say that you're a Life Coach and you want to expand your clientele, perhaps because you've been so successful that many of your clients have now left because you've helped them to lead happy, fulfilling lives. There are two ways in which Google can help you.

1 Google Search: If someone actively searches for career or personal development, your ad will appear on the results page if you've chosen your keywords carefully.

2 Google Content Network: This is slightly different, and there are more details in the Appendix. Your potential customer may not be actively searching for the service you offer, but you're placing a link to your services right in front of the very people most interested in what you're selling.

Targeting your Google ads

The beautiful thing about AdWords is that you only have to pay if someone actually clicks on your link. You only pay for people who are interested in whatever it is you're selling. Being displayed on a search results page or, to go back to our life coaching example, on a site that discusses life coaching, doesn't actually cost you a penny until someone clicks that link to your website. Brilliant, isn't it?

It would be helpful here quickly to explain a couple of terms that Google uses within AdWords to help you understand how you can make your ads maximize their potential and make you some money.

Campaign

Your Google AdWords account will be made up of a set of 'campaigns', the large themes of what you want to advertise. Examples are always helpful, so let's return to our shoe repair business. Overall the business deals with anything to do with shoe repairs, but your campaigns will include the broad themes within your business, for example, New Soles, Broken Heels, Leather Repair.

Ad Groups

Within each of your campaigns will be a series of 'Ad Groups'. In our example, the Shoe Repair campaign might include Ad Groups for heels and soles. The Heels campaign might feature Ad Groups for stilettos and kitten heels.

Within each Ad Group will be one or more ads that describe the product, for instance the soles, and may include different variations of ads describing the different soles on offer, rubber, leather etc. The keywords you choose will then help Google to decide when to show your ad following a search.

The most common way to build an ad within your Ad Group is to use a headline, a description and a link to your website. But if you're feeling adventurous, you can create graphic ad banners that will appear on Google's content network on websites that match your product or service.

Google is really good at helping you to narrow the scope of your ads and to focus on the people you want to reach. For example, you can set geographical details at the campaign level that help you target specific towns and postcodes, counties, even countries.

You can even target your ads by time of day. Let's leave our shoe repair business for now and set up a pizza service instead. If you are offering pizza deliveries, you'll want to target people in your area only. A customer in Carlisle probably won't be willing to wait five hours for a pizza from Norwich, no matter how tasty and authentically stone-baked it might be. AdWords allows you to narrow your ad to appear only to people searching from your local area.

But you can do even better than that. People are most likely to order pizzas between around 5 pm and 2 am, so you can change your AdWords settings to bid more for clicks at that time of day because they are more likely to result in a sale than someone browsing your site at 9 am.

All these methods of honing your ads to reach the serious, paying customer will help you save money on your advertising by turning a greater percentage of your clicks-through into genuine sales.

Now keep reading as I explain how you can work out exactly what you can afford to pay for those valuable clicks and how to turn browsers into buyers.

PAYING THE RIGHT AMOUNT FOR YOUR CLICKS

A common way of visualizing customer transactions on the internet is to use the analogy of a funnel. Staying with our little pizza business, let's imagine that at the top of the funnel, at the widest part, are all the people who have typed 'pizza' into a search engine and therefore triggered your ad. These are the 'impressions' of the ad; the people who have seen it, but have not yet clicked on it.

Lower down, where it becomes narrower, the funnel is populated by the number of people who did decide to click on it. A good ad will generate a click-through rate of between half a per cent and three per cent of the impressions. If just 1 per cent of all the people who see your ad click on it, you're doing pretty well.

Now you have a visitor to your site. A real potential customer. The stomach is rumbling, the lips are being licked and this customer is busy browsing your wonderfully tasty menu items and studying your reasonable prices. If that person now completes the final step and places an order, they belong in the last, most narrow part of the funnel. If you can turn 5 per cent of those visitors to your website into paying customers, then you can give yourself a big pat on the back.

So how does all this help you to work out what to pay for each click?

Let's say that on average you charge £10 for each shoe repair and the cost of the repair is £2, which leaves you a gross profit of £8 per customer. Let's build ourselves a sort of equation, based on the click-through figures we're hoping to achieve. 10,000 people see your ad, 100 will click on your ad, 5 want their shoes repaired, leaving you a profit of £40.

In effect, each one of those 100 clicks – potential customers – has been worth 40 pence. Therefore, when you make your bids for that particular ad in your Ad Group, you can spend up to 40 pence.

Now the trick is to balance your profit versus the volume of customers you want. If you bid the full 40 pence you'll get the maximum number of clicks, but no profit. If you bid 1 penny you'll get fewer clicks but you'll receive a profit of 30 pence for each one. As you get more comfortable with the amount of clicks coming from the ad you'll be able to strike a balance between the level of profit and the volume of clicks.

Those are the very basic rules, but as we have already seen with regard to targeting your ads by using the words or aiming it at different times or geographical areas, there are all kinds of ways you can optimize the effectiveness of your ads and reduce the amount you pay for each click.

Strategies for improving the quality of clicks

Make sure you're using relevant keywords to your product. If someone searches for 'ingredients for pizza' and your ad for pizza delivery appears on the results page, the searcher is unlikely to click on your link because they're researching making a pizza themselves. They're not interested in buying a shop-made pizza at that time. It's a keyword you wouldn't want to pay much for because if someone does click your site, you probably won't make a sale; you've wasted money on the click.

By the same token, a search that is much more specific, for example: 'shoe repairs in Norwich', is something you would be willing to spend more money on because the likelihood of a sale following a click will be high. This is a customer who wants what you're selling and who lives in your area, so you need him or her to click your ad rather than any pesky local competitors.

Always track the performance of your keywords. This allows you to work out whether you're overbidding for unsuccessful keywords or underbidding for more fruitful ones. Google offers a free tool, Google Analytics, that you can install on your website to help you analyse these statistics. All you need to do is to put a code on your website, which is very straightforward. The tool will then report back to you with all kinds of stats and data. As you begin to understand the numbers better and feel more comfortable using the tool, you can really start to drill down and optimize the performance of all your ads.

Once you've chosen your keywords, the next stage is to write an ad that will grab the attention of the person searching. This can be a real balancing act, because ideally you want to attract attention from a genuine potential customer while avoiding the attention of someone who might click but is unlikely to buy. For example, an ad that says: 'Free shoe repairs, all day, every day, order now!' might produce a lot of clicks, but not a lot of profit.

Twenty-five characters for the headline and 35 characters each for the two descriptive lines doesn't leave you with a great deal of scope, so be careful with your wording. Ideally, you need to provide information about your product or service followed by a call to action that really nudges people along to your site.

Time and again research has proved that a 'passive' ad is not as effective as an 'active' one. A shoe repair ad saying, 'High quality repairs, decent prices' provides information but doesn't urge the potential customer to take advantage of it. An ad that says, 'Quick service, great value, order now!' is actively encouraging people to click as well as providing them with information about the product.

Remember, wording is vital. Google doesn't allow unnecessary capital letters or more than one exclamation mark, so you must rely on the actual words to entice your customers in.

So how much should you pay?

One of the key things to accept before you start using AdWords is that it's an ongoing learning process. You'll always be seeing ways in which you can improve, methods with which you can save money, and how and why particular ads work better than others. You'll be forever fine-tuning your AdWords account to make it work for you, so don't be downhearted if at first your ads are not performing as well as you might hope. You will get there and with the help and advice from this book it won't take long.

So, before you start your AdWords campaign, try to figure out how much money you expect to make. This will help you work out how much each click is going to be worth to you. In our shoe repair example we discovered that each click was worth about £0.40, but in fact it's worth paying a little more than you're comfortable with at first because then you'll soon begin to see the results and you'll be able to react to them accordingly.

Once you start selling your shoe repair service you might realize that it's worth paying the price of a cup of coffee for the person that searches 'shoe repair in Acton' and only five pence for the person that searches for 'shoe cobbler'. It may take dozens or even hundreds of people to click onto your website before you can really discover which keywords and ads are the most successful, but eventually you'll learn the best way to attract paying customers.

It's possible with AdWords to set the price you want to pay at keyword level or Ad Group level, but do bear in mind that sometimes you can tweak too much. Take a step back once in a while. If you've made a profit of £2,000 in June and you paid £1,000 in advertising to Google for the same month, you're doing pretty well. It pays to take a look at the wider picture sometimes and not get bogged down by the tiny micro-elements of your strategy.

Finally, it's perfectly natural to worry about how much you're spending, particularly if you're running a small business. Fortunately, Google has an option that allows you to put a limit on how much you spend each month. So if you hit your maximum after three weeks, your ads will stop and you won't pay any more for that month. If this is happening, however, it's usually a strong signal that you're paying too much for each click through to your website and you'll need to adjust accordingly.

You're doing really well! Keep reading. The next chapter explains how to maintain your click-through rating and how to keep those customers safely reaching your landing page.

TOP TIPS

 Establish what kind of business you're running. Is it a product or a service? What needs are you aiming to fulfil for your customers?

 If you're unsure about your market, set up a simple web page and basic AdWords campaign to test the water.

 If you're offering a brand new product or service, focus your ads on the need you're fulfilling or the problem you're solving, not the name of your business that nobody has yet heard of.

 To help reach those potential paying customers, use AdWords' tools to target your ads to specific geographical areas or even particular times of the day.

 You can work out how much a click-through for a particular ad is worth by studying your profits and the percentage of success each ad delivers. Use Google Analytics to examine the performance of your ads.

 Specifically worded ads are more likely to result in sales because they match very specific searches. If these ads produce results, check you're bidding enough for the click-through.

 Try to include a call to action in your ads that gives people a shove towards your website. Make it active, not passive.

Question

How do you choose a trigger word?

Action

Google matches the words that someone types into the search with the words that will make your ad appear. These words don't actually have to appear in your ad, but you have chosen them because they are what your customers will be searching for and they will trigger the advertisement to appear. If you choose a popular keyword it will be more expensive than a word that is never searched for.

CHAPTER 5
SECRETS OF SUCCESSFUL ONLINE ADS

In this chapter I'll show you how you can reach your customers at the precise moment they want to buy the product or service you're offering. But, just as important as enticing people to click your ad in the first place, is maintaining your 'Click-Through Rate' (CTR) so that your ad stays as high as possible on Google's search result pages. I'll show you just how to achieve that consistency.

I'll also explain how to construct your ads to maximize your AdWords rating, using a whole range of tactics:

- telling your audience what your product or service is;

- highlighting its benefits;

- choosing the right words, the right phrases, and the right number of words and phrases;

- expanding your list of keywords;

- using online tools to help you generate variations on your keywords.

Cosmetic and plastic surgeons in California

Helene Gryfakis is a Price-per-Click Marketing Director based in the USA and she manages the AdWords account for a cosmetic and plastic surgery group in Beverly Hills, California. The company has a wide range of services including breast implants, tummy tucks, liposuction, rhinoplasty, facelifts and other plastic surgery procedures. The business uses certified plastic surgeons and also provides gastric banding for clients with weight issues and podiatry doctors for painful foot problems. Her aim was to utilize the website as a medium for generating leads for the business.

Helene discovered that key AdWords for cosmetic surgery are both expensive and competitive. The group had been using AdWords at a high cost with not much return. Words such as liposuction, breast implant, or breast augmentation were expensive and a campaign using them exhausted the budget set for each day. Helene said 'Many people were clicking on the ads but no one was buying, and the fixed sum set for marketing had run out by lunchtime each day.' The business was running through the set budget quickly in the morning and then there would be no ads running the rest of the day. The site was ranking high for non-converting keywords.

So Helene's first task was to sort through the ranking keywords and discover which ads were successful. The strategy worked well and within a month of taking over the campaign the average cost per lead dropped by almost two-thirds. Equally important, the number of potential customers doubled.

Her most important piece of advice is to develop multiple ads. She proved to the cosmetic surgery company that it's not enough to write one ad for a group of words. With one advertisement you can't compare which ad is working best and discover which ads are more compelling. So she wrote six ads for an ad group and made everyone slightly different. She suggested there should be slightly different offers, a slightly different call to action, and different wording. Then she could assess which ads have a higher click-through and conversion. Every week she would compile a list of the top performing ads and withhold the low performing ones.

What made the entire project unusual was that some of the cosmetic surgeons had appeared on popular American TV shows about plastic surgery, including programmes like *Dr 90210*, *Access Hollywood*, *Entertainment Tonight*, and *The Tyra Banks Show*. Helene realized that 'as seen on TV', or 'Dr 90210', was a less expensive AdWord than 'breast enhancement', so she began to test new AdWords based on subjects the TV programmes were featuring. Insurance issues were discussed on one programme and she would promote insurance as an element of the ads. Many plastic surgeons don't take patients using insurance, so identifying insurance as a call to action became a compelling element of the advertisement. Alternatively, she'd focus on location, and the geographical situation of the clinic in Beverly Hills became an important part of the advertisement. Another successful keyword was 'top surgeon'. As soon as one of the surgeons featured on a TV show, many of the viewers decided that he was the man to fix their problem, so they would search against the programme titles and would click to the ad featuring his name. She said, 'We'd focus on the actual surgeons because their names were high-profile. Then, through our testing, we were able to see which ads converted the best just from all the different calls to action.'

After two years of working with the cosmetic surgery group the Google Ads were fine-tuned and the cost per conversion dropped again. Helene's view is that analysing the data and adjusting daily will make a significant difference to the Cost-per-Click.

The only way you will get ahead with Google AdWords is by looking at the data every day. If you just let it run on the default, your ad is displayed but not targeted. You may get people just clicking but they don't have a serious interest. So you're paying for nothing. Checking your keywords in order to make sure each one is converting will make sure that your ad spend is cost effective.

Cosmetic surgery is a big business and soon the group discovered their competitors copied their strategy. Helene found that as soon as she had a successful ad, a competitor would copy her campaign and keywords. Her advice is to avoid bidding for the number one position, unless it's part of a particular plan, such as a short-term promotion. You save money that would simply be spent on out-bidding the competition. In her experience the customers click the first and the second advertisements, but it's the third advertisement that converts to a sale. Her analysis showed it's the place between a second and fourth position that provides serious customers for the cosmetic surgery group. And she certainly has a happy face!

All customers go through a series of stages in their mind before taking the plunge and paying for a product or service. It's what we might call the 'purchasing cycle'. Obviously, the bigger the purchase, the more thought will go into it. Someone buying a house is going to spend a lot more time considering the pros and cons than someone looking to buy a lampshade.

REACHING CUSTOMERS WHO ARE READY TO BUY

Still, there are identifiable stages common to any purchase. The cycle starts when people begin to think about a product they might need. At this stage, your ad may be of some interest to them, but they're not ready to part with their cash.

Next follows a stage of research, where potential customers will look into the product and compare costs and features and, increasingly these days, will consult opinions online from those who've bought similar products. Again, your ad will be of interest to them, but a click-through may still not result in a sale.

Finally, your potential customers reach that golden 'purchasing stage', when they have their credit or debit card glinting in their hand and they're ready to do business. This is the optimum moment when you want them to see your ad and click-through to your website. These are the people you're looking to attract and you need to make sure you're paying the right amount for that visitor to your site.

When people reach this stage, they're likely to be typing in 'trigger' words, such as 'buy', 'purchase' or 'need'. These kinds of words signal that the searcher is ready to become a paying customer, so when these words are typed alongside your kind of product, you need your ad to appear as high up the Google search results page as possible. Depending on how fierce your competition is, these words can become expensive but in the long run it's a good investment because clicks that result from these searches are far more likely to earn you a sale.

If searchers use words such as 'compare' or 'price', they're still in the research stage. Of course you want your ad to appear to these people because you want to be included in their research, but at the same time you don't want to be paying as much as you would for the key trigger words that indicate a more imminent purchase.

Once your ad appears following a juicy search you need to try every little trick to encourage people to select your ad above any other ad on the list. If your ad appears but people don't tend to click on it, Google notes this, decides that it's not relevant enough and it begins to drop down the list.

One way to grab the attention of your potential customer is to use a Google AdWords tool that allows you to replace the headline of your ad with the exact words of the relevant search. This is effective because it immediately shows searchers that you have exactly what they want.

Let's just have a look at how this works. Imagine you typed your pizza ad like this:

{KeyWord: Great Pizza}

Delicious Secret Sauce

Pepperoni Petes. Fill your tum!

PetesPizza.com

Then, if someone searched for 'Norwich Pizza Delivery', the ad would appear on the results page like this:

Norwich Pizza Delivery

Delicious Secret Sauce

Pepperoni Petes. Fill your tum!

PetesPizza.com

It's the same ad, but it's been individually tailored to the person who typed the search, making it more attractive. If the search term is greater than the 25 characters allowed, then the ad simply reverts to your original 'Great Pizza' headline.

Use your words carefully. Be succinct and clear and, as we discussed in the last chapter, remember that all-important 'call to action', which has a really significant effect on how a potential customer reacts to an ad. Don't be shy of highlighting the benefits of your product in your ad. If your pizza is the cheapest in the area, say it. If you use a special tomato sauce passed down from your Italian ancestors, let people know. But just find a way of saying it in five or six words. Use punchy, interesting phrases that will make your ad stand out from the crowd.

EXPANDING YOUR LIST OF KEYWORDS

Once you've written your first ad and you've chosen a couple of keywords, the next stage is to expand your list and start finding ways of reaching more and more potential customers.

Let's say that one of the keywords you've chosen for your pizza business is simply, 'pizza'. This is a common internet search word because pizza is a popular food item that people are willing to order online. But if someone simply types in that single word as a search, they could be typing it for any number of reasons. They might want to know how to make pizza, the average calorie count of a Hawaiian pizza, where they can buy frozen pizza or they may even be researching the origins of this wonderful Italian food. Are you feeling as hungry as I am?

The point is that people who type such a broad search may not be interested in buying a takeaway pizza at all. That's not to say you shouldn't run an ad with that keyword, but because you can't possibly be sure what the searcher is after, it's not worth paying a lot of money for it.

The point of your ad is to attract as many profitable clicks as possible, so your aim has to be to gather all the words you can think of that someone who wants to buy a take-away pizza might type into Google. One way might be to use the word 'pizza' in combination with all the different toppings you offer, 'pizza pepperoni', 'pizza mushrooms', 'pizza vegetarian', 'pizza meat lovers', and so on. You're trying to match more specific searches; searches that are likely to result in sales.

Next you could consider the different styles of pizza on offer, like 'deep dish pizza', 'filled-crust pizza', or 'authentic stone-baked pizza'. And if you're really smart you may be able to find a little niche area that no one has thought of that doesn't contain your main keyword, whether that's pizza, watch repair or life coaching. Perhaps you might include a keyword for 'garlic bread' or, for those real Italian aficionados you want to target, how about 'calzone'? The advantage of finding niche words that other companies might not think of using is that you won't need to pay so much to get your ad at the top of the results page.

Slowly, you can expand your keywords in this way and eventually graduate to using three-or-four-word keyword combinations that can be very profitable. Let's just break this down a bit so you can see what I mean:

Keyword: Pizza: This is very general and unlikely to result in a sale.

Keyword: Pepperoni pizza: This is better. It's more specific and shows the searcher has a little more idea about what he or she's after.

Keyword: Buy pepperoni pizza: Now we're getting somewhere. What you have here is someone willing to buy a pizza. You can comfortably pay more for this search because the likelihood of a sale is higher.

Keyword: Buy Pepperoni Pizza in Norwich: This is perfect, as long as your business is in Norwich. You have a hungry customer in your area who wants pizza. Naturally, this is a search that won't appear as often as simply 'pizza', but your click-through rates and conversion to sales rates are going to be much higher. Your service is exactly relevant to the search, so you can bid more money and stand a much better chance of appearing at the top of Google's results page. Remember, it's safe to bid higher because you don't pay Google anything unless someone clicks on your link.

As your list expands, you'll be able to tell which ads are netting you the most profits and which are not performing quite so well and, accordingly, adjust the prices you're paying for clicks. It's just as important to pay the right price for your clicks as it is to get your clicks in the first place.

Helpful tools

Thinking up all those keywords may sound a little tough. It's not. You don't need to sit there for hours racking your brain for all the different variations that fit your product, because happily Google is here to help. Simply click the 'Keyword Tool' button in your AdWords account and type in your first keyword – for example, 'pizza'. This helpful tool will immediately report back to you with all kinds of synonyms and variations and similar words that people may type into a search engine when looking to buy a pizza.

Private companies can offer a similar kind of service along with further analysis and useful statistics that will help you choose the perfect words for your ad. Usually these services offer a free trial for a limited time so you can decide for yourself how handy for your needs their service might be.

One example is Word Tracker, which helps you understand the kind of volume of searches particular words receive. For instance, you might discover that the word 'pizza' is receiving 37 million global searches, with around two-thirds of them in America, while 'Italian pizza' is getting just 90,000 searches. Once more, it's clear that being specific pays dividends. 'Pizza' gets millions of searches and your small business may be lost in the shuffle, but 'Italian pizza' is more of a niche that your business may be able to take advantage of.

Another site worth visiting is Keyword Discovery, which can help you research words that perform successfully and can suggest alternative terms or phrases you may not have considered.

So you can see there are two quite distinct skills to creating something approaching the perfect ad. The first is the creative part, where you attempt to write a clever, punchy ad that will outshine your competitors, and the second is the analytical side of locating the right keywords, honing them, and discovering the exact amount of cash you should pay for each individual click. Once you've finished reading this book, you'll be an expert in both.

MAINTAINING THE QUALITY OF YOUR AD

As we discussed in the last chapter, Google offers a lot of clever little tricks that allow you to narrow down your audience and to target, as far as possible, those most likely to buy your product. When a search is made, Google can identify roughly the area where the computer is located, so you can instruct AdWords to show your ad only to people in your immediate area, or you can limit the times of day when you want your ad to appear.

But there are more factors that count towards your ad's positioning on the results page than how much you pay and the relevance of your keywords. Google's system is intuitive, smart and powerful and is able to study the correlation between the wording on your ad and the wording on the web page that your ad links to.

For example, let's say that your pizza ad shows as follows:

Great Pizza

Best quality pepperoni

Quick service, buy now!

PetesPizza.com

Now, if the web page on your site that this ad sends the customer to is actually a page about pasta then there's a 'disconnect' between what the ad is claiming and what the page is actually about. Even though your site sells great quality pepperoni pizza, if the page you are sending people to doesn't mention it, then Google will lower your quality score and it can cost you a high spot on the results page.

However, if your link takes customers to a page that explains just why your pepperoni is the best and lists your variety of pepperoni pizzas and the prices, Google will give you a higher quality score for your landing page and your ad will remain prominent on the results page.

Think carefully about the ads you're buying. If you run a very small website, ensure that all your ads are relevant to the information on your site. If you have a larger website, you can be very specific about which pages you direct people to. For example, if a person is searching for vegetarian pizza, make sure your ad for veggie pizzas has a link that directs them to your specialist veggie-pizza-only page.

Keep everything tight and relevant and Google will reward your honesty. Remember, Google is interested in serving its customers the best way it can. It's not interested in advertisers who fool people into visiting sites that don't contain the kind of information they're looking for.

Google wants people to get what they want as simply as possible. And that's what you want too. So be as helpful as you can in guiding people to the right parts of your site.

TOP TIPS

 Customers who type in 'trigger' words such as 'buy' or 'purchase' into a search engine are most likely to become paying customers, so make sure you bid high for those clicks.

 If people are seeing your ad but are not clicking on it, Google calculates that it's not useful to its users and so drops it down the list. If this happens, consider dropping the ad altogether, since it's not having the effect you're looking for.

 Try using the {KeyWord:} to allow the headline of your ad to be replaced by the exact wording of a relevant search. It's a great way really to grab the attention of a potential customer.

 Don't be afraid to emphasize the benefits of your product in your ad.

Expand your keywords to include all the different words, phrases and permutations someone might type into Google if they're interested in buying your product or service.

To establish your own advertising niche, try to find words that your competitors may not think of using. This can be surprisingly effective and is also likely to be cheaper than relying on common, established, words.

Matching specific keywords to specific searches maximizes the chances of attracting a customer ready to make a purchase.

Utilize online tools such as Adwords' Keyword Tool or Word Tracker to help you think of new keywords and study the effectiveness of different words and phrases.

Always ensure that your ad and the web page your ad links to are relevant to each other. Google will then keep your quality score nice and high.

Question

How many advertisements have you created?

Action

Make more than one advertisement. You need to compare which ad is working best so make each one slightly different. Then you can assess which ads have a higher click through to your website, and which ads create a sale. When you know which ads work best you can remove the ones that don't work. Remember that you only have to pay when someone uses your advertisement to click through to your site, so the only cost of creating more advertisements is the time you spend.

CHAPTER 6
SECRETS OF CREATING A GREAT CAMPAIGN

You want your website to be 'hot'. You want people to want to come to your site and to want to buy your product or service. To achieve this takes time and your website needs to be developed in line with the traffic you are driving to it. In this chapter we'll explore together a number of techniques for creating, analysing and managing the wealth of data produced by AdWords.

I'll reveal the secrets behind developing your AdWords strategies to maintain and then grow the number of visitors to your website. Your AdWords campaigns need to be continually altered and refined to create the best results.

There are three simple steps to achieve this:

- Set up your campaigns.

- Set up your initial bids for clicks.

- Manage your bids to get the best performance from your ads.

One of the wonderful advantages of AdWords is its flexibility and your ability to be equally flexible, to change to fit the needs of the market, will be the key to your success. This chapter will explain how to manage the data that results from the performance of your ads and how to alter your ads, your keywords and your bids.

As we saw a little earlier, it's commonplace for a company to set up a simple web page to test the waters for a particular market, and in this chapter I'll explain in a little more detail how you can do this.

CASE STUDY

Managing a campaign – engineering an electoral victory

The Obama election campaign

If you're a current affairs junkie you might have noticed how political parties are using the internet to increase support amongst their potential voters. Probably the best known example in the political world is the Obama US Presidential election campaign in 2008. Political pundits looking back at the election now say that what they term 'online advocacy' was a key reason for Obama's success. Much has been written about the social networking side of Obama's online campaign for victory, but could it be possible that the Democrats also used AdWords? The campaign leaders realized there is no point in posting an interesting website if no one can find it. The Obama campaign team was advised by lots of top new-media executives including Eric Schmidt, CEO of Google, so presumably they really understood how to make AdWords work for them.

The Obama campaign team were using the information I've already given you in this book:

- Only 10 per cent of the people who find a website through Google search will click on a site further than the first page of search results.

- So it's best to be on the first page of the search results in order to be found.

- Up to a third of Google search users don't understand the difference between the results that have not been paid for and the sponsored search results, the ones where a business has paid for a click on a keyword.

So how did they use these three key bits of information? Well, first they developed websites which were named, that is the URL of the site, with popular search words to increase the chance they would appear at the top of the search results. The websites contained information the voters would be interested in. If they used Google to search, then the Obama site was under a popular keyword and by paying more for that keyword the campaign team made sure the Obama website was in the top ten on the search page.

Then, because they knew there would be anti-Obama campaigning online, they looked out for anything negative and obtained Google keywords that would take the searcher to the negative material. At the same time they created Obama-friendly material under the same keywords they had bought. Then, if searchers found the keyword, there'd be an equal chance that they'd move to the Obama positive website rather than the negative story online. So up-beat stories about Obama were easy to find and helped his team keep a positive online presence throughout the campaign.

Finally, throughout the political campaign the team worked hard to understand their potential voters; to fit-in with the needs of the electorate they would change the keywords they used. They never stood still but kept looking to see what words delivered the results they wanted. It worked; the online activities engaged the electorate. Obama swept to power, and the result, as they say, is history.

The key to squeezing the most out of your AdWords campaigns is managing and studying your data. How many impressions are your ads getting? How many clicks are you receiving? What's the conversion rate of click-to-sale? How much are you paying for each click and for each sale?

For many businesses the problem is it can take some time to build up a large enough pile of statistics before you can start drawing some solid conclusions. So which type of business is likely to produce data more quickly; which kind of business is AdWords best tailored to fit? And how well will your business respond to an AdWords campaign?

DEVELOPING A CAMPAIGN

Which businesses are most suitable for an AdWords campaign? Well, the answer is that any kind of service or product that can be fulfilled online, where a customer can research it and purchase it with an online transaction, can give you quick feedback on how well your product is faring in the marketplace. As we've seen, the product can even be a political party. In fact information products are good examples, but anything that involves a product being bought online and then shipped to a customer will also show results pretty quickly.

The sale of flowers is a useful model here. There are a lot of ads online offering a service of delivering flowers and it works well as an internet business because it's straight-forward and immediate. A customer can find the website, browse the different arrangements and then place an order. The flowers can be delivered the same day, the next day or on a different specified date, but the transaction is completed and the service carried out without the customer having to go through all the hassle of visiting a flower shop and transporting a bouquet to the recipient. Because the entire process is instantaneous, it becomes a business that can rack up stats and information very quickly.

You can apply this to almost any physical product you like, but it's worth bearing in mind that with items of clothing or footwear particularly, but even with products such as electronics, the return rate when selling online can be pretty high. So one thing you need to guard against is happily counting up all your money without taking into account the percentage of customers that change their minds and want their money back.

Services that can only be performed offline are a little more difficult to track and it might be tough to link your AdWords campaigns to the success or otherwise of your business. Abandoning our pizza parlour for a moment, let's imagine you've decided to roll up your sleeves and develop the best car wash facility in town. High-pressure water hoses, top quality sponges, smooth chamois leathers and a wax and polish service that'll make even the most battered old banger twinkle in the sunlight. You get the drift.

You may begin your AdWords campaigns with the idea that people will see your ad and, as a result, drive down to your premises to receive the full treatment for a very reasonable price. But it'll be very difficult for you to know whether your customers are coming because they saw your ad, or because a friend told them about your service, or because they were simply driving past and realised their car was filthy and could do with a clean. It makes it tough to work out just how much you should pay for each click because you can't ever be sure you're converting clicks to customers.

You can, of course, work on ways to help improve this, perhaps by offering a 10 per cent discount for customers who book their car in for a wash by sending an email or by printing out a voucher, but you can never be as sure about your results as you can with a more immediate product such as flowers.

Testing the water

Google AdWords is a tremendous tool for researching a potential market for a new business. As I mentioned a little earlier, there's nothing to stop you setting up a small one-or-two page website, beginning an AdWords campaign, and then studying your volume of clicks and working out how much those clicks are likely to cost you.

It's something you can set up remarkably quickly and run for a few days. For example, imagine you're setting up a flower shop in a small town. Your website could be a single page with some useful information about the imminent debut of the new venture, such as:

- the name of the business;
- some basic contact details;
- information on the kind of occasions your flower arrangements can cover;
- how quickly flowers can be delivered;
- details of a special opening week promotion.

You can run the ads and the website for a few days, using your special keywords and asking Google to show your ads only to people searching in your geographical area. Quite quickly, you could start to develop an idea of the volume of clicks your business might receive. You're not completely misleading the people searching because you hope in the future they might return to take advantage of your service. If the ads are not delivering a lot of volume then you might want to reconsider the business, but if you are receiving a lot of hits then you may have struck gold.

Naturally, this won't produce data as accurate as the real business will deliver, but it will give you a decent idea of the kind of market out there and how effective your concept might be.

Paying for your ads

When you begin your first AdWords campaign, Google will suggest a fairly high price to start with. This will help ensure you have a decent spot on the search results page and you can start receiving the volume of clicks your business needs to get going. Remember, though, to set a daily spending limit on your campaign.

Even if you're testing a few basic keywords to see how they might perform, you need to stop thinking in terms of a cup of coffee or a pair of shoes, and rather the cost of a new suit. Much less than that and you won't really be testing your idea stringently enough or giving it enough chance to succeed.

But if your ads are receiving plenty of clicks thanks to your attractive copy and your smart targeting, and if the relevance to the page you're directing people to is high, then Google will begin to rate your ad highly because it's delivering what Google users need. Once that happens, you'll start to receive a discount on your ads.

Let's return to our new flower business. Your ad might read something like:

Beautiful Flowers
Fast, reliable delivery
All occasions, order now!
Flos-Flowers.com

The keywords you might be targeting would be something like: 'quick flower delivery', or 'immediate flowers'. This is a competitive business, so it might cost you perhaps the price of a cup of coffee per click. At this stage, Google doesn't know how relevant or how good your ad might be until after a few days of receiving dozens or even hundreds of clicks, Google will begin to calculate that your ad is rather effective. So you have to be prepared to make an investment here.

This is great news because if Google is impressed with the quality of your ad it'll give it a boost in the rankings *without any increase in the price you're paying*. It's the beauty of AdWords; you're rewarded for your smart wording and attention to relevance as well as the money you're willing to invest.

If your original ad was sixth on the list on the search results page, you might see it boosted to second or third if it's performing well and obviously the higher your ad in the rankings, the more clicks you'll receive and the more business you'll get.

And then you can start to make a bit of a calculation yourself. If the amount of business you were getting while your ad was placed sixth was actually pretty high, you might decide to reduce your bid for each click and keep your ad in that sixth position because you don't feel you need to be top of the rankings to make your business work.

MANAGING YOUR DATA

A common mistake when it comes to altering your campaigns, whether it's the wording of your ads, the choice of keywords, or the amount you're paying for clicks, is to make decisions before enough data is available.

If your ad is receiving one or two clicks per day then it's dangerous to start making changes because you can't be sure those clicks are representative of your potential clientele. A good rule of thumb is to wait until you have at least a hundred clicks on an ad before making any changes, otherwise you're guessing what is working rather than relying on hard data.

Yet again, however, Google is here to help, particularly when you're starting out. It's easy to be unsure about the wording of your ad in these early times and you'll have understandable doubts, so a good strategy is to write ten different ads and feed them into the AdWords system. Within these ads you can try different words, different phrases, different combinations, and experiment with that all-important call-to-action. Google will then rotate those ads for you on the results pages. Over a period of time it'll work out which ones are performing best and start to use those ads above the ones that have been less successful.

It's a service that doesn't cost you any extra money, because, as always, you only pay for actual clicks to your website.

Your AdWords Account is made up of your campaigns and each campaign has a daily spending limit. Within those campaigns you have your ad groups and each group has a set of keywords and a set of ads to run against them. A maximum of 50 ads per group is a decent number to test with and once you have some results, you can begin to delete the ones that have performed poorly.

The problem is that it can take a lot of time to collect enough data on an individual keyword to decide whether you should persist with it or how much you should be bidding for it. The solution is to bid for a group of keywords so that you can reach a larger chunk of data faster than you would for an individual keyword.

Let's use our flower shop again to illustrate the point. Within one ad group you decide to use the keywords: 'fast flower delivery', 'immediate flower delivery' and 'quick flower delivery'. These are all similar keywords. For the first you might receive 40 clicks, for the second you might receive 20 clicks and for the third you might get another 40 clicks. Individually, there's not really enough there to make an informed decision on how well they're working, but if you add them together in the same ad group you have 100 clicks. That means you can set an accurate bid for the ad group as a whole and it'll apply to all your keywords in the group. In effect, you're pooling your data to allow you to make a smarter decision on the investment you're making in your ads.

Then you can start to burrow even deeper. Try to keep keywords that perform similarly in one ad group. For instance, if 'immediate flower delivery' is netting you a high rate of conversions to actual sales, but 'fast flower delivery' is receiving a lower conversion rate, nip 'fast flower delivery' out of that ad group and build another group based around the word 'fast'; one you can bid a little less for.

These seemingly small changes can really save you money.

Once you've set up your ads and you're beginning to see positive results, you may not need to manage them quite so strictly. If the ads are producing sales, it might just need the odd little tweak here and there to keep the ship steady, but largely Google will handle all the heavy lifting and you can sit back with a cup of tea and give yourself a pat on the back for an ad well written.

Even then, it pays to keep an eye out for particular fads and trends that might end up driving extra business your way. A sudden heat-wave might see a sharp rise in sales of sandals, for example, so an online shoe shop might quickly run a new ad:

Cool your feet!

Summer Sandals are here

Next day delivery, order now

SheilaShoes.com

Other events, of course, you'll be able to see coming. With our flower shop all it would need is a brief check on the calendar.

Mother's Day,14th March. This is always a date that flower shops thrive on, so perhaps even in January you might decide to start running ads for Mother's Day flower deliveries. Then you can start being really clever because the link on your ad could take a customer to a page with a series of special Mother's Day offers, which will please Google for its relevance and therefore keep your ad nice and high in the rankings.

Gathering data about your customers

As your business continues to gather pace you can begin to think about using your website to capture additional data about the people who visit. One way is to encourage visitors to leave their e-mail address or phone number so they can be contacted with regard to special offers or deals.

Another is to use a video clip or a sound clip that people can learn more about your product or service. You can monitor how well such an application is performing by the number of downloads it receives. It's all part of developing your website and becoming truly focused on fulfilling your customers' needs to the letter.

The whole process around AdWords relies on you being flexible and imaginative and willing to try all the different tricks I've explained throughout this book. So what are you waiting for? Get out there and start making AdWords work for you!

TOP TIPS

A business where a full transaction can take place online will be in a better position to utilize the data generated by AdWords than a business that requires offline activity.

Be prepared to invest an initial few hundred pounds in your AdWords campaign to give your ads a chance of succeeding.

An ad that's popular and relevant will end up saving you money because Google will give it a boost in the rankings due to its effectiveness.

Wait until you receive at least 100 clicks on an ad before chopping and changing your wording. Receiving one sale from one click doesn't tell you anything; the next 99 clicks may yield no sales at all.

You can ask AdWords to rotate a new set of ads and work out itself which are the most effective.

Group sets of similar keywords together in one Ad Group so you can accumulate useful data about their performance more quickly and make an informed decision about the amount you should be paying for a click.

Keep your eyes peeled for topical fads or relevant dates in the calendar – you might want to produce limited-time ads to cash in on them.

Question

How much are you going to spend on your advertising campaign?

Action

You need to start with a slightly high price for your advertisement so that you have a high spot on the search results. You will get clicks through to your website enabling you to see how many of the people who visit will buy your product. Once you have some traffic to your site you can reduce the price, and try different words that people will use to search for your products. Always set a limit with Google of how much you are prepared to spend per month, week or even per day.

APPENDIX

INTRODUCTION

There's no need to start reading this until you've already got up and running with Google AdWords. You can test the demand for your business idea with a simple one page website, so only move ahead with web design, part one of this appendix, when you're certain you can make some money from your idea. If you're moving down the design route, then you may well want to use banner advertisements as well as Google AdWords, and the second section gives you some quick tips and Ad-vice about how to manage this. The third section of the appendix is analytics, which really means measuring how well you're doing. If you read the story of the shoe company then you'll understand how it works. Section four has a short case study about creating content as well as ads, which can be another revenue earner. Then, under part five I've concluded with a thought that you might want to explore other search engines.

1 DESIGNING YOUR WEBSITE

Once you've equipped yourself with a domain name and web address, the next step is to decide how you want to go about designing your website.

Building a website can cost anything from a few pounds to thousands. If you've decided to do-it-yourself, and there are many sites on the internet that will give you advice on how to do this; the costs are minimal. The domain name hosting company is likely to be a one-stop shop, in that they will also, for a few pounds more, lease you web space, provide you with simple templates for your web pages, and help you set up a dedicated e-mail address to go with the site. There'll be tools that help you choose different designs and change the colours or the fonts, as well as enter the text. This'll give you a basic, though not especially exciting, website.

If you want a website with a few more bells and whistles, one that's more individual, you'll need to access custom web pages HTML, a process by which you go outside the template, edit the page yourself and change the look and feel more extensively. This, though, is much more compli-cated than following the template system, and you'll need to learn how to do it. Making it look good takes practice, and a fair eye for design.

Without a doubt, creating a website yourself is the cheapest way of doing it. But before you decide on this money-saving route, pause a moment to assess your skills and abilities honestly, as well as what you want from the website. Certainly it's not difficult to set up a basic website for yourself. But there can be a world of difference between a basic website and a good one. There's absolutely no point in spending just a few pounds to cobble together your own website if it irritates you by looking amateurish, and doesn't do the job you want it to.

The alternative to building your own site is to contact one of the many small firms who do web page design for businesses. They'll rapidly set you up with a professional page that contains all the right links and content you'll need to support your business. Before you choose which firm to use, ask them to provide you with a list of websites they've built, and surf the internet to look at them to see if you like the style, and how well they work.

A less proficient website design will drag on and wander. It'll look amateurish, perhaps too many quirky typefaces on one page, backgrounds that don't enhance the foreground content, too many headings and links, a hallway with too many interconnecting doors, in which it's possible to lose yourself and never find what you're seeking.

The most professional websites will feel much crisper. The imagery will be distinctive, and not have the look of a template that's used over and over again on other sites. There'll be an element of real design. Visitors will know immediately that this has been professionally put together.

2   BANNER ADS

Even though Google is the largest search engine online it doesn't mean you can ignore the rest of the internet where there are millions of websites waiting for you to advertise your products. If you want larger distribution and awareness for your business, then your own ad banners on pages all over the web could create a wider presence.

Before you consider creating ad banners, you need to think about whether they're appropriate to your business. If your product is visual, then banners can be more effective than a word search. Imagine you ran an amusement park with roller coasters and rides; pictures of happy children are going to convey more than a written description. So if I see a picture of an amusement park I might think about taking my daughter there for the weekend even though I'm not necessarily searching for amusement parks. A theme park is the kind of product that people click to on an impulse rather than searching for, and banner ads are different from a search result because they promote impulse clicks.

Banner ads are harder to create because you don't know exactly what sites they'll be displayed on, and furthermore an image banner has more variables to consider than a three-line text advertisement. More detail about this follows, but you have to think about the images on the banner as well as the text placement. So a banner ad is harder to perfect, and it takes a lot longer to create. A good designer might develop two or three great image banners in a day, whereas, as I've shown you in this book, anyone can create 50 or 100 text ads in a day. If you're running a one-man/woman business then my advice is to start by using the Google templates. If, however, you're serious about banner advertisement on content network you'll need a professional designer in the future.

Quick Start to banner ads

1 Use the AdWords tool and templates to create some simple banners.

2 Follow the same techniques as when you created the search text ads.

3 Choose an interesting image, something that'll catch people's eye and get their attention.

4 Write a small amount of explanatory text, building up some intrigue or getting the person interested in your product.

5 Have a clear 'call to action' such as, 'Get a free quote', or 'Click here', or 'Join now', on the button.

TOP TIPS

 Many banners are fronted with a human face. If you have a human face on the banner, especially if it's looking out, the viewer's eye will almost always take a look. Sometimes there's a funny expression or sometimes the person is very pretty; faces are very powerful. If you don't have suitable pictures, you can buy them online from a stock photograph library.

 Don't put too much information on your banner. You want to create interest in your product so people click through to your website.

 Your website should relate to the banner. If you had a pretty girl doing gardening on your ad banner, the landing page people come to should repeat that image. A consistent message tells customers they've come to the right place when they made that click.

Cost of clicks on banner ads

Google assigns quality scores to your banner ad and to your landing pages. As your banner ad starts to get clicks, its quality is proven and you'll pay less for the same amount of traffic. The common mistake is to bid too low at the beginning and not get traffic to your banner ad and then give up.

You have to start out willing to spend a little bit more than you might be comfortable with paying in the long term. However, once Google realizes the quality of your ad and the landing pages they'll reduce the amount you'll have to pay and that's when your ad starts to become much more effective.

What size banner?

There are six main sizes, all measured in pixels, which are used on the internet, and the different sizes have different performance characteristics.

The best performing is the square 250×250 pixels banner. Web users have become used to the long skinny ad at the top or at the side of the page and don't pay much attention to them. The square banner is more intrusive and takes up more of the page, so people are more likely to notice it.

Other main sizes:

- the 300×250 which is called the inline rectangle;

- the 728×90, which is the skinny long banner that you see at the top of many websites, called the leader board;

- the 120×600 is called a skyscraper. That's the skinny banner which goes on the right hand side of the page;

- the 160×600, which is the slightly fatter banner, and is called a wide skyscraper.

Tools

Click on the tools button to either add your own image, as described earlier, or you use the tool Display Ad Builder which will give you a set of different templates to look through.

Choose the template you want, it's very simple, and Google will create the Ad in all the different sizes so you can look at what works best for your product. Once you've chosen the size, Google wants to know in which ad group you plan to place your banner. So you choose the campaign or ad group where you want it to run. Give your banner ad a name so you can remember what it is in the future, as you may find that you have lots of ads.

Now you're back with tasks similar to AdWords. Google asks for a headline, which you want to keep short and attention-grabbing. If you have an image of your product you can upload it. You then label the button. It could say 'Learn more', it could say 'Have fun today', it could say 'Get a free quote', whatever it says, remember it should be action-oriented, and just enough brief text to get people to click. Finally, there's a section to put in the URL of your website. You can choose how much of the URL you want to reveal on the banner, so you can just show the website name, but ensure that the click goes directly to a landing page of your choice.

How much does it cost?

You choose the price, or set the bid, you plan to pay for the ad at the ad group level.

Let's assume you're still running the amusement park with roller coasters, so maybe for your amusement park you'll have a roller coaster ad group and a water ride ad group. For the water rides ad group, you could bid at £0.20 per click for when the ad is placed in and around content about amusement for children. Google will show all of the ads you've created for water rides at the £0.20 price and will determine which one works the best and show it more often. Google is excellent at helping you figure out which is the best ad and then running more of them.

When creating ad banners in Google, best practice is to create new ad groups that are only for the ad banners, because they behave differently from keywords. Google will try to match the ad banners to websites with similar content.

TOP TIPS

 When people type in a search they're actively looking for something and ready to purchase; there will be higher click-through rates and searchers are more likely to become customers.

 Ad banners appear everywhere and when people click on them it's more to do with impulsiveness and curiosity; they're not in the same frame of mind as when they're in the buying cycle. Even though they visit your website, the likelihood of them actually buying your product or service is still much less than from the search keywords.

3   ANALYTICS

Google is a very scientific company and everything is based around numbers and analysis. If you click into the standard AdWords Campaign Manager you'll find a good reporting system that tells you about clicks and impressions and how well your different ads are doing; but it doesn't tell you a lot about how your actual website is performing. If you want further information on that you can turn to Google Analytics. This is a very simple to use web analytics tool and it's free. Sign up for it inside your AdWords account in the reporting area and add some very simple pieces of HTML to your website.

CASE STUDY

Analytics

Schuh is a shoe shop with 65 stores on the UK high street and a big website that sells footwear online. Schuhstore.co.uk gets around 400,000 different visitors each month and has increased the number of people buying shoes on its site by a few simple techniques. Schuh use Google information to discover what parts of the site the customers have visited and are continually upgrading and changing the site so that customers can use it better. They believe that sales, marketing, IT and finance are all part of the same function, having the objective of improving the customers' experience so they buy more shoes.

Schuh's basic approach is to test its own website continually and change it to make sure it works for the customers. People buy more than one pair of shoes in a lifetime, so Schuh plan to sell to each customer more than just once. Ideally they would like what they call 'life-time' value from each customer, and for that they need answers to some simple questions.

- Does the website work?
- Does the link take people to where they want to go?
- Does it give them the shoes they want to buy?

Because Schuh have actual stores as well as a virtual one on a website, they've taken the expertise from their shop to the online experience. They know that shoes don't sell in a cluttered shop, so they don't clutter the site. Just as the place to pay is easy to find in the shop, so the check out is easy to find on the website. They don't make customers fill in forms before letting them buy shoes in the shop, so they don't bother them online either. The online experience is closely connected to the actual stores; you can buy online and take the item back to any Schuh store, check stock availability in any of the stores, online, and have stock transferred from branch to branch.

Schuh think their customers know what they want. If they've come to the site through Google AdWords they're already searching for a pair of shoes. So they're enticed with special offers and a call to action such as 'Sale' or 'Buy Now'. Schuh's basic rule is that all ads must lead to a page with the product on it because shoe shoppers will leave if they don't immediately see what they're searching for. Schuh has found it's the small improvements that make the difference, and their sales are growing.

Schuh have worked with Google UK to try to come up with more effective ways of helping customers. They aim for what the Google website calls conversion. Google describes conversion as something that 'occurs when a user completes an action on your site that you consider to be valuable. This can be making a purchase, downloading a file or requesting additional information.' Conversions can be seasonal in the shoe business. For example, not many people hunt for boots in the summer, or for sandals in the winter. Schuh use the analytics Insights for Search seasonal trends button with a wide date range, like '2005 – now', to see when search volume is highest. It shows that at Christmas, Schuh's best selling items are Ugg boots and trainers.

Google has a Conversion Optimizer that allows Schuh to specify a maximum cost-per-acquisition (CPA) bid. This represents the most they want to pay for each shoe sale from their site. Using information from the site, the Conversion Optimizer then predicts, in real time, which clicks are most likely to result in a conversion. Based on these predictions, the Conversion Optimizer sets higher CPC bids for more valuable clicks and lower CPC bids for less valuable clicks. Schuh worked out the maximum amount they wanted to spend on each sale or lead before advertising costs meant they wouldn't be making a decent profit. The amount changed from product to product; expensive leather boots had a higher CPA than plastic flip-flops. Sometimes they increase the CPA just to see if that will lead to more sales of the expensive boots with their bigger profit margin than the cheaper flip-flops. What's interesting is that the Schuh team are keeping an eagle eye on what's selling and why.

Schuh continuously update and improve the website and use the Website Optimizer tool to test which pages of their site work best. They wanted to know, for instance, whether customers were more likely to buy shoes when shown a big picture or if they were equally motivated by smaller pictures. They created alternative versions of the test page with a big and with a small picture. The Website Optimizer showed each of the alternative versions to different visitors. The two different page variations took the shopper to the checkout where they could buy the shoes, and Schuh discovered which picture led to most sales.

If you place the analytics tool on the key pages of the website, it will start tracking everyone who visits and it can start giving you information about:

- what country they come from;
- sometimes what county or city they come from;
- how long they stay on the website;
- whether they just saw one page and went away;
- whether they saw lots of pages.

If you want more in-depth information, you can tie the analytics to actual purchases. It can tell you the volume and the value purchased as well as what pages purchasers see before they buy. It can even tell you how big is the screen someone is surfing the internet on, so you can tell whether you need to make your web page work well on a small screen or whether it's okay to make it fill up the whole of a big screen. It can tell you, too, whether people are using a dial-up modem or broadband connection.

Analytics can also give you a lot of information about how the different keywords perform. Much of this information is in the basic AdWords feedback, but Analytics has a deeper and better interface for looking at how certain keywords perform over time, such as whether they just got people to come and look or whether they actually motivated a purchase. It's a very powerful tool.

Quick Start for Analytics; this should take 30 minutes

Go to the **Reports** tab in your AdWords account, which will take you through the steps for setting it up. The basic steps for setting it up are to add a little piece of code to your website.

Download the code. Add it to your web pages and that's all there is to it. If you put the code in the header and footer of the web pages, then it'll appear on every page of the website. Once that code is on your website, all the tracking will start to happen and it will immediately flow back to your analytics account.

The results will be shown to you in a panel, a dashboard, which shows you how your traffic has done over the last few days. There's a graph that shows you whether your traffic's high or low. It shows you where your traffic is coming from on a map of the world and you can drill in and get more detail on any of these areas.

Traffic sources

Analytics can tell you whether people are finding your website direct, in other words somebody is typing in your website because they've heard of you, or whether they're coming from search engines. If they're coming from search engines are they coming from Yahoo or Google and are they paid or non-paid? What we've been talking about so far in the book is all about paid AdWords traffic, but there's also the non-paid. If you come up in the free results, called organic, that's significant too. If you drill down even further, it can tell you the words people are typing in to actually find you and that's very helpful in figuring out which AdWords work best for your business.

TOP TIPS

 Don't start making decisions with too little information.

 Depending on how big your website is and how much traffic it generates, there's interesting information coming in to analytics every day and you may have information you can act on.

 But don't rush to change things until you can see a pattern.

4 ADSENSE

Google AdSense is a Google programme based on content rather than on search.

Google AdSense: Rock Jock

Geoff runs a gay-themed fitness site called Rock Jock. It contains fitness tips and information about fitness programmes with a gay/lesbian slant. AdSense runs alongside the information.

So, if you're selling Lycra clothing to people who like to exercise in comfortable, figure-hugging clothing, and you've set up your AdWords ad to show on the content network, your ad will appear on the Rock Jock pages if Google thinks it's relevant to Rock Jock's content. Every time a visitor to the Rock Jock site clicks on your ad, Google will charge you a fee and 50 per cent of it will go to Rock Jock because they created the attractive content.

Website owners who sign up for AdSense can display Google ads on their websites and receive money for any clicks on the ads. Instead of Googlebot, Google uses a different web crawler, Mediabot, to crawl web pages to analyse content. It then places ads specifically related to the content onto those pages. Google's content network has become the largest network of advertising sites in the world. When you sign up for AdWords, if you tick the box saying 'show this on the content network', then the same ad will automatically go out on the content network.

This means your ad will appear on websites within the network that discuss issues surrounding personal development. Your potential customers may not be actively searching for the service you offer, but now, while they browse this website, they'll be faced with your ad. Effectively, you're placing a link to your services right in front of the very people most likely to want to hire you; those already interested in or researching the subject and who would find your products relevant.

5   ADS ON OTHER SEARCH ENGINES

Google AdWords is the best place to get your feet wet and to understand exactly how online advertising can benefit your business. The tools and help available are the best on the market and it's the easiest to set up.

Once you believe you have a real grip on AdWords and you're satisfied with the performance of your ads, you can look into further options. The lessons you've learnt with AdWords will be applicable to Google's competitors such as Yahoo! and Bing, although it's worth remembering that Google has 80 per cent of the market.